The Weekly Meal Plan
COOKBOOK

The Weekly Meal Plan
COOKBOOK

A 3-Month Kickstart Guide
to **Healthy Home Cooking**

Kylie Perrotti

creator of TriedAndTrueRecipe.com

Skyhorse Publishing

Skyhorse Publishing books may be purchased in bulk at special discounts for sales promotion, corporate gifts, fund-raising, or educational purposes. Special editions can also be created to specifications. For details, contact the Special Sales Department, Skyhorse Publishing, 307 West 36th Street, 11th Floor, New York, NY 10018 or info@skyhorsepublishing.com.

Skyhorse® and Skyhorse Publishing® are registered trademarks of Skyhorse Publishing, Inc.®, a Delaware corporation.

Visit our website at www.skyhorsepublishing.com.

10 9 8 7 6 5 4 3 2 1

Library of Congress Cataloging-in-Publication Data is available on file.

Cover design by Daniel Brount
Cover photo by Kylie Perrotti

Print ISBN: 978-1-5107-4607-7
Ebook ISBN: 978-1-5107-4608-4

Printed in China

This book is dedicated to my parents, Jim and Barbara Thompson, for inspiring me to cook throughout my life; my husband, Jason Perrotti, for always supporting my dreams; and my cat, Grammy, for always being with me in the kitchen while I cook. I also owe a great deal of gratitude to my best friends Chrissy Marselle and Marci Yankelov for always being listening (and collaborative) ears to my never-ending supply of ideas.

Contents

INTRODUCTION

I am a self-taught home cook who started a cooking blog (TriedAndTrueRecipe.com) because
I wanted a no-frills, no-nonsense approach to finding easy, elegant, and delicious meals to make
at home. I had a growing catalog of recipes, but what about people who wanted something even
simpler? I began to imagine all the different scenarios where someone may not want to dig through
even one cooking blog—a busy mom or dad who has to plan seven dinners each week *and* shop for
them, a novice cook who wants to elevate their home cooking but feels overwhelmed, or someone
who likes to cook but is sick of buying a full bunch of basil only to use a few leaves for one recipe as
the rest slowly wilts in their fridge.

And so, *The Weekly Meal Plan Cookbook* was born!

The goal of this book is to take the guesswork out of planning with a comprehensive grocery list,
reusable and easy-to-source ingredients, and simple recipes for beginner home cooks. Each week's
grocery list is organized by store department, allowing you to buy all your ingredients for the week
in one shopping trip. Many of those same ingredients or "key players" are used in multiple recipes
throughout the week, so home chefs never have to throw away half-used basil again.

PLAN 1: WEEK 1

This seven-day recipe plan includes dinner recipes for five days, all of which serve four. To conquer the grocery store in one shopping trip, the next page outlines a detailed grocery list, with items separated by store department. You will also find storage, freezing, and thawing tips to help you plan your week. This plan focuses on bright, clean flavors paired with simple cooking techniques—such as roasting and poaching—to allow the brightness of the lemons and fresh parsley to shine through. Pay special attention to the key players throughout the week (butternut squash, flat-leaf parsley, and fresh lemons) and be sure to buy the freshest and healthiest of those ingredients that you can find, because you will use them for multiple recipes. Store produce in a bag in the crisper to keep fresh.

THE MENU

MONDAY
Chicken and Butternut Squash Soup with Crispy Squash Seeds

TUESDAY
Poached Fish with Roasted Vegetables

WEDNESDAY
Spicy Turkey Sausage Orecchiette

THURSDAY
Vegetarian Lentil Salad with Roasted Butternut Squash and Mozzarella

FRIDAY
Roasted Pork Tenderloin with Herbed Pearl Couscous

PLAN 1: WEEK 1
CONQUERING THE GROCERY STORE

FOOD SAFETY GUIDELINES

Buying groceries for the entire week can require some forethought, so be sure to refer to the FDA's storage and freezing guidelines for raw ingredients. All fish, chicken, and steak require twenty-four hours to thaw out in the fridge.

Raw fish, shellfish, chicken, and ground meats: Store in fridge for 1–2 days
Steak and pork (roasts and chops): Store in fridge for 3–5 days
Uncooked, unopened bacon: Store in fridge for 1–2 weeks

MEAT & SEAFOOD

- ☐ 1 pound ground chicken
- ☐ 4 (4-ounce) cod fillets
- ☐ 1 pound ground spicy or mild turkey sausage
- ☐ 1 pound pork tenderloin

GRAIN

- ☐ 16 ounces orecchiette
- ☐ 2 cups pearl couscous

OIL

- ☐ Cooking oil
- ☐ Extra-virgin olive oil

DAIRY

- ☐ 1 cup heavy cream
- ☐ 2 tablespoons butter
- ☐ 1 (8-ounce) ball of fresh mozzarella

STOCK

- ☐ 8 cups low-sodium chicken stock
- ☐ 3 cups low-sodium vegetable stock

FRUITS & VEGETABLES

- ☐ 3 yellow onions
- ☐ 2 medium butternut squash
- ☐ 4 medium Yukon Gold potatoes
- ☐ 2 zucchinis
- ☐ 3 lemons
- ☐ ¾ cup fresh flat-leaf parsley
- ☐ 5 scallions
- ☐ 5 ounces arugula
- ☐ 10 ounces baby spinach
- ☐ 8 ounces cremini mushrooms
- ☐ 1 red bell pepper

PANTRY & SPICES

- ☐ 1 (15-ounce) can black beans
- ☐ 1 (14.5-ounce) can fire-roasted crushed tomatoes
- ☐ 1 (14.5-ounce) can crushed tomatoes
- ☐ ½ cup walnuts
- ☐ 1 cup dry green lentils
- ☐ Paprika
- ☐ Cumin
- ☐ Chili powder
- ☐ Garlic powder

- ☐ Cayenne powder
- ☐ Dark brown sugar
- ☐ Sugar
- ☐ Dry rosemary

- ☐ Salt
- ☐ Pepper
- ☐ Crushed red pepper

TIP

To speed up the thawing process, place the frozen protein in a resealable storage bag and push out the air before sealing the bag. Place the bag in a bowl and run cold water over the bag. Fill the bowl with water and use a heavy jar (such as peanut butter) to keep the bag submerged below the water. Replace the water every ten minutes with more cold water. Alternatively, allow the water to run at a very slow rate. This will take anywhere from thirty minutes to an hour. Note: To keep bacteria from forming, the water must be at 40°F. If using standing water, do not allow the water to reach room temperature.

Chicken and Butternut Squash Soup
with Crispy Squash Seeds

Time to Make: 50 minutes

Serves: 4

WHY THIS RECIPE WORKS

Instead of discarding the butternut squash seeds, this recipe quickly dries them out and roasts them for a crunchy topping.

SUBSTITUTIONS

Ground chicken: Ground turkey, ground beef, ground bison, or more butternut squash and an additional can of black beans

Butternut squash: Acorn squash or sweet potatoes

Heavy Cream: Omit, if preferred

EQUIPMENT & LEFTOVERS

You'll need: Soup pot, fine-mesh sieve, paper towels, baking sheet

Leftovers: Store leftovers in the fridge for 3–4 days

INGREDIENTS

2 tablespoons paprika

2 tablespoons cumin

1 tablespoon chili powder

2 teaspoons garlic powder

1 whole medium butternut squash, trimmed, peeled, and halved lengthwise, seeds scooped out and reserved

3 teaspoons cooking oil, divided

1 pound ground chicken

Salt and pepper to taste

1 yellow onion, peeled and diced

4 cups low-sodium chicken stock

1 (14.5-ounce) can fire-roasted crushed tomatoes

1 (15-ounce) can black beans, drained and rinsed

Cayenne powder to taste

1 tablespoon dark brown sugar

2 teaspoons extra-virgin olive oil

½ cup heavy cream

(Continued on next page)

METHOD

1. **Prepare the spice blend:** In a small bowl, combine paprika, cumin, chili powder, and garlic powder.

2. **Prepare the squash seeds:** Preheat oven to 350°F. Separate the butternut squash seeds from the stringy squash fibers and rinse them until they are clean in a fine-mesh sieve. Lay them out on paper towels and pat them dry. Allow the seeds to dry on paper towels as you prepare the rest of the recipe.

3. **Cook the chicken:** Heat 2 teaspoons cooking oil in a soup pot over medium-high until very hot. Add the chicken and season with salt and pepper. Cook 5 minutes until the chicken begins to brown. Add half the spice blend and stir to combine. Continue cooking until well-browned and cooked through, about 5 minutes more. Scoop the chicken out and transfer to a bowl.

4. **Prepare the soup base:** Add remaining 1 teaspoon cooking oil to the soup pot over medium heat. Add diced onion and cook, stirring often, until the onions begin to soften, about 5 minutes. Add 1 cup of the chicken stock and scrape up any browned bits stuck to the bottom of the pot. Add the butternut squash and toss to combine before pouring in the rest of the stock along with the crushed tomatoes and black beans. Stir to combine.

5. **Season the soup:** Bring the soup to a boil and season with salt, pepper, cayenne powder, and the remaining spice blend. Stir in the brown sugar. Reduce heat and simmer for about 20 minutes or until the squash is fork tender.

6. **Prepare the squash seeds:** As the soup is simmering, toss the reserved squash seeds with a pinch of salt, pepper, and 2 teaspoons extra-virgin olive oil. Arrange the seeds in an even layer on a baking sheet or in a small oven-safe skillet. Transfer to the oven and bake for 10 to 15 minutes, turning the seeds once halfway through cooking. Watch the seeds carefully so they don't burn. Remove from the oven and set aside.

7. **Before serving:** Stir the heavy cream into the soup and taste and season to your preferences.

8. **To serve:** Divide the soup between bowls and garnish with the crispy squash seeds. Enjoy!

Poached Fish with Roasted Vegetables

Time to Make: 35–40 minutes

Serves: 4

WHY THIS RECIPE WORKS

Poaching is a simple yet effective technique for buttery, tender fish. This recipe allows you to prepare the broth and fish as the vegetables roast. Lemon juice and butter are added to the broth right before serving for brightness and richness that complement the roasted vegetables and the delicate poached fish.

SUBSTITUTIONS

Cod: Hake, haddock, halibut, or another firm whitefish

Zucchini: Eggplant, yellow squash, or chopped broccolini

Baby spinach: Arugula, watercress, or baby kale

EQUIPMENT & LEFTOVERS

You'll need: Paper towel, baking sheet, wide sauté pan, aluminum foil, zester

Leftovers: Store leftovers in the fridge for up to 3 days

INGREDIENTS

4 medium Yukon Gold potatoes, diced into 1-inch cubes

2 zucchini, trimmed and diced into 1-inch cubes

2 tablespoons cooking oil

Salt and pepper to taste

3 cups low-sodium vegetable stock

1 (14.5-ounce) can crushed tomatoes

Crushed red pepper to taste

Pinch sugar

4 (4-ounce) cod fillets

2 tablespoons butter

5 ounces baby spinach

¼ cup fresh parsley, roughly chopped, a pinch reserved for garnish

1 lemon, juice and zest

(Continued on page 9)

METHOD

1. **Roast the vegetables:** Preheat oven to 425°F. Transfer the potatoes and zucchini to a foil-lined baking sheet and toss with 2 tablespoons oil. Season with salt and pepper. Transfer to the oven and bake for 20 to 30 minutes, flipping once halfway through. Remove from the oven.

2. **Prepare the broth and fish:** While the vegetables are roasting, in a wide sauté pan bring the vegetable stock and crushed tomatoes to a boil. Season with salt, pepper, crushed red pepper, and a pinch of sugar. Boil for 8 to 10 minutes or until just beginning to reduce. Turn the heat to low and add the fish. Cover and cook for 10 to 12 minutes or until fillets are opaque and cooked through. Using a slotted spoon or spatula, carefully transfer the fish to a plate and cover with foil to keep warm.

3. **Finish the broth:** Bring the poaching broth back to a boil for 5 additional minutes. Stir in butter, spinach, and all but a pinch of parsley leaves. Pour in the lemon juice. Taste the broth and season with salt, pepper, and crushed red pepper to taste.

4. **To serve:** Spoon the roasted vegetables into shallow bowls and place a fish fillet on top. Ladle the broth over each dish. Sprinkle with lemon zest and the reserved chopped parsley and a sprinkle of crushed red pepper, if desired. Enjoy!

Spicy Turkey Sausage Orecchiette

Time to Make: 40 minutes

Serves: 4

WHY THIS RECIPE WORKS

Spicy, creamy, and full of flavor, this spicy turkey sausage orecchiette is the perfect weeknight indulgence. Best of all, this recipe is easy to prepare, and it is easy to substitute ingredients depending on your preferences.

SUBSTITUTIONS

Orecchiette: Any small pasta, such as shells, farfalle, or orzo

Turkey sausage: Pork sausage, ground beef, ground bison, ground turkey, broccoli florets, or omit

Cremini mushrooms: Shiitake mushrooms or diced eggplant

Baby spinach: Arugula, watercress, or baby kale

Heavy cream: Omit, if preferred

EQUIPMENT & LEFTOVERS

You'll need: Large pot, large skillet

Leftovers: Store in the fridge for 3–4 days

INGREDIENTS

16 ounces orecchiette

1 tablespoon cooking oil

1 pound loose spicy or mild turkey sausage

8 ounces cremini mushrooms, scrubbed and sliced

1 red bell pepper, trimmed, deseeded, and diced

1 yellow onion, peeled and diced

Salt and pepper to taste

1 cup low-sodium chicken stock

½ cup heavy cream

½ teaspoon paprika

¼ teaspoon garlic powder

¼ teaspoon cayenne powder

5 ounces baby spinach

¼ cup fresh parsley, roughly chopped, a pinch reserved for garnish

(Continued on next page)

METHOD

1. **Prepare the pasta:** Bring a large pot of salted water to a boil and cook the pasta according to the instructions. Reserve ½ cup cooking water and then drain and rinse the pasta.

2. **Cook the sausage:** Heat cooking oil in a large skillet (large enough to later hold the pasta) over medium-high heat until very hot. Add the sausage and cook for 10 to 12 minutes, breaking up with a wooden spoon, until the sausage is completely cooked through. Use a slotted spoon to remove the sausage from the skillet and transfer to a bowl.

3. **Sauté the vegetables:** Add the mushrooms to the skillet and cook for 5 minutes or until just beginning to soften. Add the bell pepper and onion to the skillet with the mushrooms and season the vegetables with salt and pepper. Cook for 8 to 10 minutes or until the bell peppers are beginning to char and the mushrooms are a deep golden brown. Add the sausage back to the skillet.

4. **Prepare the sauce:** Pour chicken stock into the skillet and scrape up any browned bits stuck to the bottom. Bring to a boil and then reduce heat. Add the heavy cream along with paprika, garlic powder, and cayenne powder. Season to taste with salt and pepper.

5. **Finish the pasta:** Pour in the reserved cooking water and stir to incorporate. Add the spinach, fresh parsley, then the cooked pasta, and toss to combine. Once the spinach is just wilted but still bright green, turn off the heat.

6. **To serve:** Spoon the pasta into shallow bowls and sprinkle the reserved parsley leaves over each dish. Enjoy!

Vegetarian Lentil Salad
with Roasted Butternut Squash and Mozzarella

Time to Make: 35 minutes

Serves: 4

WHY THIS RECIPE WORKS

Tender, not mushy, lentils are paired with a simple, bright lemon dressing while roasted butternut squash adds depth and warmth. These ingredients are complemented by freshly torn mozzarella that adds the perfect amount of richness.

SUBSTITUTIONS

Green lentils: Black lentils, barley, brown rice, or quinoa (cook times may vary)

Butternut squash: Acorn squash or sweet potatoes

Arugula: Baby spinach, watercress, or torn kale leaves

Fresh mozzarella: Crumbled goat cheese or fresh ricotta

EQUIPMENT & LEFTOVERS

You'll need: Saucepan with lid, baking sheet

Leftovers: If you are planning on enjoying leftovers, keep the arugula separate from the lentils. The salad, sans arugula, can be made 2 days ahead of time.

INGREDIENTS

1 cup dry green lentils

3 cups water

Salt to taste

1 medium butternut squash, peeled, deseeded, and diced

Pepper to taste

1 tablespoon cooking oil

½ cup walnuts, roughly chopped

1 tablespoon extra-virgin olive oil plus extra for serving

1 lemon, juice

Crushed red pepper to taste

5 ounces arugula

1 (8-ounce) ball of fresh mozzarella

Fresh cracked black pepper, optional, for serving

(Continued on page 15)

METHOD

1. **Prepare the lentils:** Clean and sort dry lentils before cooking. Combine the lentils and 3 cups water in a saucepan with a sprinkle of salt. Bring to a boil and then reduce to a gentle simmer and keep covered for about 20 to 25 minutes or until tender but not mushy. Drain and rinse under cool water and season with a generous sprinkle of salt. *Note: Do not salt the lentils while they're cooking.*

2. **Roast the squash:** Preheat oven to 400°F. Toss the squash on a baking sheet with 1 tablespoon of cooking oil and salt and pepper. Transfer to the oven and roast for about 25 minutes, turning once halfway through cooking. Five minutes before removing the squash from the oven, sprinkle the walnuts over the squash and roast until warm and toasted. Remove from the oven.

3. **Prepare the arugula:** In a large bowl, whisk together 1 tablespoon extra-virgin olive oil along with the lemon juice. Season with salt, pepper, and a sprinkle of crushed red pepper. Add the arugula and toss to coat. Next, add cooked green lentils and the warm butternut squash and toss to combine.

4. **To serve:** Divide the lentil salad between bowls. Tear the mozzarella into bite-size pieces and arrange on top of each salad. Drizzle each salad with a touch of extra-virgin olive oil and a crack of fresh black pepper, if desired. Enjoy!

Roasted Pork Tenderloin with Herbed Pearl Couscous

Time to Make: 35 minutes

Serves: 4

WHY THIS RECIPE WORKS

Although the ingredients may be simple, this recipe has plenty of flavor. Toasting the couscous adds a wonderful nutty flavor to the sautéed vegetables.

SUBSTITUTIONS

Pork tenderloin: Boneless pork chops, chicken breasts, cauliflower steaks, or large-diced squash

Pearl couscous: Quinoa or fregola

EQUIPMENT & LEFTOVERS

You'll need: Paper towel, oven-safe skillet, wide sauté pan, zester

Leftovers: Store in the fridge for 3–4 days

INGREDIENTS

1 pound pork tenderloin

Salt and pepper to taste

2 tablespoons cooking oil, divided

1 yellow onion, peeled and minced

1 teaspoon dry rosemary

5 scallions, trimmed and minced, a pinch
    reserved for garnish

2 cups pearl couscous

3 cups low-sodium chicken stock

¼ cup fresh parsley, roughly chopped, a pinch
    reserved for garnish

1 lemon, juice and zest

Extra-virgin olive oil, optional, for serving

METHOD

1. **Prepare the pork:** Preheat oven to 400°F. Pat the pork dry and season all over with salt and pepper. Heat 1 tablespoon oil in an oven-safe skillet over medium-high until very hot. Add the pork tenderloin and cook for 3 to 4 minutes per side. Transfer to the oven for 12 to 15 minutes or until instant-read thermometer reaches 140–145°F for medium rare. Rest for 5 minutes and then slice the pork.

2. **Prepare the couscous:** In a wide sauté pan, heat the remaining 1 tablespoon oil over medium-high heat until very hot. Add the minced onion and cook, stirring regularly, for 1 to 2 minutes or until just beginning to soften and brown. Add the dry rosemary and minced scallions and cook for 45 seconds or until fragrant. Pour in the pearl couscous and cook, stirring regularly, for 3 to 5 minutes or until the couscous begins to turn golden brown. Add chicken stock, season with salt and pepper, and then bring to a boil. Reduce heat, cover, and simmer for 10 minutes or until the couscous has absorbed all the liquid and is tender. Turn off the heat.

3. **Finish the couscous:** Fold in parsley, lemon juice, and lemon zest and stir to combine. Taste and season with salt and pepper.

4. **To serve:** Thinly slice the pork tenderloin. Spoon the couscous onto plates and arrange the sliced pork tenderloin on top. Garnish each dish with the reserved scallion greens and chopped parsley. Drizzle each dish with a touch of extra-virgin olive oil, if desired. Enjoy!

PLAN 1: WEEK 2

This seven-day recipe plan includes dinner recipes for five days, all of which serve four. To conquer the grocery store in one shopping trip, the next page outlines a detailed grocery list, with items separated by store department. You will also find storage, freezing, and thawing tips to help you plan your week. This plan focuses on big, bold flavors with unique sweet and savory pairings, such as spicy red lentils with sweet golden raisins and sweet and candied carrots paired with walnuts and creamy mozzarella. Pay special attention to the key players throughout the week (arugula, fresh ginger, and red onions) and be sure to buy the freshest and healthiest of those ingredients that you can find, because you will use them for multiple recipes. Store produce in a bag in the crisper to keep fresh.

THE MENU

MONDAY
Sweet and Spicy Red Lentils with
Wild Rice and Greens

TUESDAY
One-Pot Spicy Shrimp, Tomatoes, and
Cannellini Beans

WEDNESDAY
Pork Tenderloin with Fresh Broccoli
and Quinoa Salad

THURSDAY
Vegan Mushroom Noodle Soup

FRIDAY
Roasted Carrot Salad with Arugula
and Walnuts

PLAN 1: WEEK 2
CONQUERING THE GROCERY STORE

FOOD SAFETY GUIDELINES

Buying groceries for the entire week can require some forethought, so be sure to refer to the FDA's storage and freezing guidelines for raw ingredients. All fish, chicken, and steak require twenty-four hours to thaw out in the fridge.

Raw fish, shellfish, chicken, and ground meats: Store in fridge for 1–2 days
Steak and pork (roasts and chops): Store in fridge for 3–5 days
Uncooked, unopened bacon: Store in fridge for 1–2 weeks

PROTEIN
- ☐ 1 pound large shrimp, peeled and deveined, tails left on or off depending on preference
- ☐ 1 pound pork tenderloin

GRAIN
- ☐ 1 cup uncooked white, brown, wild, or blend of rice
- ☐ 1 cup uncooked quinoa
- ☐ 16 ounces Asian noodles of your choice

OIL
- ☐ Cooking oil
- ☐ Extra-virgin olive oil

DAIRY
- ☐ ½ cup Greek yogurt
- ☐ 1 (8-ounce) ball of fresh mozzarella

STOCK
- ☐ 12 cups low-sodium vegetable stock

FRUITS & VEGETABLES
- ☐ 1 yellow onion

- ☐ 3 red onions
- ☐ 2 shallots
- ☐ 1 (4-inch) piece of ginger
- ☐ 2 heads garlic
- ☐ 2 lemons
- ☐ 1 pound fresh broccoli
- ☐ 2 medium red bell peppers
- ☐ 8 ounces cremini mushrooms
- ☐ 6 scallions
- ☐ 5 ounces baby spinach
- ☐ 15 ounces arugula
- ☐ 1 pound carrots
- ☐ ¼ cup cilantro leaves, optional
- ☐ Microgreens, cilantro, or bean sprouts, optional

(Continued on next page)

PANTRY & SPICES

- ☐ 2 (14.5-ounce) cans of cannellini beans
- ☐ 1 (14.5-ounce) can crushed tomatoes
- ☐ 1 (28-ounce) can crushed tomatoes
- ☐ 1 (15-ounce) can chickpeas
- ☐ 2 cups dry red lentils
- ☐ 1½ cups golden raisins
- ☐ 1 cup chopped walnuts
- ☐ Tomato paste
- ☐ Mayonnaise
- ☐ Distilled white vinegar
- ☐ Sesame oil
- ☐ Shaoxing cooking wine
- ☐ Soy sauce
- ☐ Sambal oolek
- ☐ Maple syrup
- ☐ Mustard seeds, optional
- ☐ Ground cumin
- ☐ Turmeric
- ☐ Cayenne powder
- ☐ Sugar
- ☐ Paprika
- ☐ Salt
- ☐ Pepper
- ☐ Crusty bread, optional

TIP

To speed up the thawing process, place the frozen protein in a resealable storage bag and push out the air before sealing the bag. Place the bag in a bowl and run cold water over the bag. Fill the bowl with water and use a heavy jar (such as peanut butter) to keep the bag submerged below the water. Replace the water every ten minutes with more cold water. Alternatively, allow the water to run at a very slow rate. This will take anywhere from thirty minutes to an hour. Note: To keep bacteria from forming, the water must be at 40°F. If using standing water, do not allow the water to reach room temperature.

Sweet and Spicy Red Lentils with Wild Rice and Greens

Time to Make: 50 minutes

Serves: 4

WHY THIS RECIPE WORKS

Golden raisins add just the right amount of sweetness to this filling sweet-and-spicy lentil dish. Serving the lentils over brown rice makes for a hearty, filling meal.

SUBSTITUTIONS

Red lentils: Yellow or brown lentils or 2 (15-ounce) cans drained, rinsed chickpeas

Greek yogurt: 1 (5.4-ounce) can coconut cream, ½ cup heavy cream, or omit

Golden raisins: Black raisins, dried cranberries, chopped, dried apricots, or chopped, dried, pitted dates

EQUIPMENT & LEFTOVERS

You'll need: Large pot, fine-mesh sieve, medium saucepan with lid

Leftovers: Store leftovers in the fridge for 3–4 days

INGREDIENTS

1 tablespoon cooking oil

1 teaspoon mustard seeds, optional

1 medium red onion, peeled and small-diced

1-inch piece of ginger, peeled and minced

1 teaspoon ground cumin

1 teaspoon turmeric

1 teaspoon cayenne powder or more or less to taste

5 cloves garlic, peeled and minced

2 cups dry red lentils

1 (28-ounce) can crushed tomatoes

4 cups low-sodium vegetable stock

Salt and pepper to taste

1 cup golden raisins

1 cup uncooked white, brown, wild, or blend of rice

5 ounces arugula

1 teaspoon extra-virgin olive oil

½ cup Greek yogurt

¼ cup cilantro leaves, optional, for garnish

(Continued on page 23)

METHOD

1. **Cook the vegetables:** Heat 1 tablespoon cooking oil in a large pot over medium-high heat. Add mustard seeds, if using, and cook for 1 to 2 minutes or until they begin to pop. Add the red onion and ginger and cook until beginning to brown and soften, about 5 minutes. Add the cumin, turmeric, cayenne powder, and garlic and cook for 45 seconds until fragrant.

2. **Prepare the lentils:** Clean and sort dry lentils before cooking. Rinse the lentils in a sieve. Pour the tomatoes and stock into the pot, add in the lentils, and stir to combine. Season with salt and pepper, then add the golden raisins. Bring to a boil, then reduce heat, cover, and cook for 30 minutes or until the lentils are very tender, adding more water if necessary.

3. **Prepare the rice:** While the lentils are simmering, prepare the rice according to package instructions in a medium saucepan with a lid. Turn off heat, remove the lid, place the greens on top, drizzle with 1 teaspoon extra-virgin olive oil, and season with salt and pepper. Return the lid to the pot for 2 to 3 minutes or until greens begin to wilt from the steam. Toss the greens in the rice until fully wilted and warm. Remove from heat.

4. **Finish the lentils:** Stir the Greek yogurt into the lentils until combined and remove from heat.

5. **To serve:** Divide the rice and greens between bowls and spoon the lentils on top. Serve with fresh cilantro leaves sprinkled on top. Enjoy!

One-Pot Spicy Shrimp, Tomatoes, and Cannellini Beans

Time to Make: 35–40 minutes

Serves: 4

WHY THIS RECIPE WORKS

This recipe is a simple, one-pot meal that gets its flavor from plenty of garlic and crushed red pepper and its brightness from the lemon juice added right before serving.

SUBSTITUTIONS

Shrimp: 1 pound cod or other firm whitefish

EQUIPMENT & LEFTOVERS

You'll need: Paper towel, wide pot

Leftovers: Store leftovers in the fridge for up to 3 days

INGREDIENTS

2 teaspoons cooking oil

1 yellow onion, peeled and diced

2 medium red bell peppers, trimmed, deseeded, and thinly sliced

1 large head of garlic, peeled and minced, divided

2 tablespoons tomato paste

2 cups low-sodium vegetable stock

1 (14.5-ounce) can crushed tomatoes

2 (14.5-ounce) cans of cannellini beans, drained and rinsed

1 teaspoon sugar

Salt, pepper, and crushed red pepper to taste

1 pound large shrimp, peeled and deveined, tails left on or off depending on preference

1 teaspoon cayenne powder

1 teaspoon paprika

5 ounces arugula

1 small lemon, juiced

Crusty bread, toasted, optional for serving

METHOD

1. **Prepare the broth base:** In a wide pot, heat 2 teaspoons cooking oil over medium-high until very hot. Add the yellow onion and sliced red bell peppers and cook until the peppers begin to soften, about 5 minutes. Add half the garlic and cook, stirring frequently, until very fragrant, about 1 minute more. Add the tomato paste and cook for 1 to 2 minutes or until it begins to deepen in color. Add vegetable stock and bring to a boil. Stir to incorporate the tomato paste into the stock. Pour in the crushed tomatoes and cannellini beans and season to taste with 1 teaspoon sugar, salt, pepper, and crushed red pepper. Reduce heat to low and simmer for 15 minutes to allow the flavors to meld.

2. **Prepare the shrimp:** In the bowl of shrimp, add 1 teaspoon cayenne powder and 1 teaspoon paprika, along with the remaining garlic. Season with salt and pepper and toss to coat. Chill the shrimp in the fridge while the broth simmers.

3. **Cook the shrimp:** Stir the prepared shrimp and arugula into the broth. Cook over low heat for 5–6 minutes or until the shrimp are opaque and cooked through and the arugula is wilted. Be careful not to overcook the shrimp. Stir the lemon juice into the pot and remove from heat.

4. **To serve:** Divide the shrimp and beans between bowls. Enjoy with toasted bread, if desired.

Pork Tenderloin with Roasted Broccoli and Quinoa Salad

Time to Make: 30 minutes

Serves: 4

WHY THIS RECIPE WORKS

The base of the broccoli salad is bright, sweet, and so easy to prepare as the pork and quinoa both cook. Thinly slicing the stems of the broccoli adds more crunchy texture contrast and ensures that the entire head of broccoli is used.

SUBSTITUTIONS

Pork tenderloin: Boneless, skinless chicken breasts or pork chops (cook time may vary)

Broccoli: Raw cauliflower, roasted sweet potatoes, or butternut squash

EQUIPMENT & LEFTOVERS

You'll need: Oven-safe skillet, fine-mesh sieve, saucepan with lid, large bowl

Leftovers: Store the pork and salad in separate leftover containers. Pork will last 3–4 days, and the salad will last up to 3 days.

INGREDIENTS

1 tablespoon cooking oil
1 pound pork tenderloin
Salt and pepper to taste
1 cup quinoa
1 cup mayonnaise
¼ cup distilled white vinegar
¼ cup granulated sugar
Dash of paprika or cayenne powder, optional
1 pound fresh broccoli
½ cup chopped walnuts
½ cup golden raisins

METHOD

1. **Prepare the pork tenderloin:** Preheat oven to 400°F. Heat 1 tablespoon cooking oil over medium-high heat until very hot in an oven-safe skillet. Pat the pork dry and season all over with salt and pepper. Once the oil is hot, add the pork tenderloin and cook for about 3 to 4 minutes per side until browned all over. Transfer to the oven for 12 to 15 minutes or until instant-read thermometer reaches 140–145°F for medium rare. Rest for 5 minutes and then slice the pork.

2. **Prepare the quinoa:** First, rinse the 1 cup quinoa in a fine-mesh sieve. Next, combine the rinsed quinoa with 2 cups water and ½ teaspoon salt and bring to a boil in a saucepan. Reduce, cover, and simmer for 15 minutes or until all the water is absorbed. Turn off the heat and let stand for 5 minutes, covered, before fluffing with a fork.

3. **Prepare the dressing:** While the pork is roasting, prepare the dressing. In a large bowl, whisk together the mayonnaise, white vinegar, sugar, and a dash of paprika or cayenne if desired. Taste and season with salt and pepper.

4. **Prepare the salad:** Trim about ½ inch at the bottom of the stem of broccoli and discard. Cut the stems from the crowns and very thinly slice the stems and transfer to the bowl of dressing. Next, cut the broccoli crowns into florets and transfer to

(Continued on next page)

the bowl with the stems and dressing. Place the walnuts in a bag and lightly crush with a few taps of a rolling pin or heavy-bottomed pan. Reserve 1 tablespoon of the walnuts and transfer the remaining walnuts to the bowl of broccoli. Add the golden raisins to the bowl. Add the cooked quinoa to the bowl of dressing and broccoli and toss to combine everything. Taste and season with salt and pepper and transfer to the fridge.

5. **To serve:** Spoon the broccoli salad onto plates and serve with the sliced pork tenderloin. Sprinkle the reserved walnuts on top of each dish. Enjoy!

Vegan Mushroom Noodle Soup

Time to Make: 30 minutes

Serves: 4

WHY THIS RECIPE WORKS

One of the best parts of this mushroom noodle soup is the garnishes. We top it with crisp microgreens—though you can omit or use fresh cilantro or bean sprouts instead—and we drizzle a simple, homemade ginger-shallot oil on top. This recipe is extremely versatile, so any leftover or extra vegetables you have such as broccoli or red bell peppers will be a perfect addition to this warming soup.

SUBSTITUTIONS

Noodles: Soba, udon, or chow mein

Cremini mushrooms: Any mushroom variety

Shaoxing cooking wine: Mirin, rice vinegar, or omit

Sambal oolek: Sriracha

EQUIPMENT & LEFTOVERS

You'll Need: Two large pots, small saucepan, colander

Leftovers: Store leftovers in the fridge for 3–4 days

INGREDIENTS

Mushroom Noodle Soup Broth

1 tablespoon cooking oil

2 red onions, peeled and thinly sliced

5 cloves garlic, peeled and minced

1-inch piece of ginger, peeled and minced

8 ounces cremini mushrooms, scrubbed and sliced

1 teaspoon sesame oil

6 cups low-sodium vegetable stock

2 tablespoons Shaoxing cooking wine

1 tablespoon soy sauce plus more if desired

1 heaping tablespoon sambal oolek

Salt and pepper to taste

5 ounces baby spinach

6 scallions, trimmed and minced, divided

16 ounces noodles of your choice

Microgreens, cilantro, or bean sprouts, optional for garnish

Ginger-Shallot Oil

⅓ cup cooking oil

2-inch piece of ginger, peeled and sliced

2 shallots, peeled and quartered

(Continued on page 31)

METHOD

1. **Prepare the mushroom noodle soup broth:** In a large pot, heat 1 tablespoon cooking oil over medium heat until hot. Add the sliced onion, and cook, stirring occasionally, for 5 minutes until softened and beginning to brown. Add garlic and ginger and cook for 1 minute, until fragrant. Add sliced mushrooms to the pot and add 1 teaspoon sesame oil. Cook, stirring occasionally, for 6 to 8 minutes or until the mushrooms begin to soften and darken around the edges. Pour the vegetable stock into the pot and scrape up anything stuck to the bottom. Bring to a boil. Stir in the Shaoxing cooking wine, soy sauce, and sambal oolek. Reduce heat to medium and cook over a low boil for about 20 minutes. Taste and season with salt and pepper to your preferences. Right before serving, reduce heat to low and stir in baby spinach and half the minced scallions. Simmer over low heat until ready to serve.

2. **Prepare the ginger-shallot oil:** While the broth is cooking, prepare the ginger-shallot oil. Combine the oil, ginger, and shallots in a small saucepan and turn the heat to medium. Once the oil begins to bubble, turn the heat down to the lowest setting. Allow to cook in the oil for about 10 minutes or until the ginger and shallots begin to darken around the edges. Stir often, taking care not to burn the ginger. Turn off the heat and allow the ginger and shallots to continue cooking in the hot oil. Stir the remaining half of the scallions into the oil and set aside.

3. **Cook noodles:** Bring a large pot of water to a boil and add the noodles. Cook according to package instructions. Drain and rinse and set aside.

4. **To serve:** Divide the noodles between bowls and ladle the mushroom broth over top. Place the microgreens on top, if using. Drizzle the ginger-shallot oil★ over the dish. Enjoy!

★Ginger and shallot are in the oil for flavor; do not plate on the dish.

Roasted Carrot Salad with Arugula and Walnuts

Time to Make: 25 minutes

Serves: 4

WHY THIS RECIPE WORKS

This roasted carrot salad is a delicious and light dinner option. The fresh mozzarella adds richness to the dish while the seasoned chickpeas add heartiness and brightness. The "candied" carrots and walnuts bring everything together with warmth and a touch of sweetness for a perfectly balanced salad.

SUBSTITUTIONS

Carrots: Sweet potatoes or butternut squash (cook time may vary)

Fresh mozzarella: Crumbled goat cheese or blue cheese

Chickpeas: Navy beans or cooked green lentils

EQUIPMENT & LEFTOVERS

You'll need: 1 sheet pan

Leftovers: Store ingredients separately in the fridge for up to 3 days

INGREDIENTS

1 pound carrots, peeled and sliced diagonally into
   1-inch-thick slices

3 teaspoons extra-virgin olive oil, divided

Salt and pepper to taste

½ cup walnuts, roughly chopped

3 tablespoons maple syrup

1 lemon, juice, divided

1 (15-ounce) can chickpeas, drained and rinsed

½ teaspoon cayenne powder

½ teaspoon paprika

5 ounces arugula

1 (8-ounce) ball of fresh mozzarella

Extra-virgin olive oil, optional, for serving

Flaky sea salt, optional, for serving

METHOD

1. **Prepare the carrots:** Preheat oven to 400°F. Toss the carrots with 2 teaspoons extra-virgin olive oil on a sheet pan and season with salt and pepper. Transfer to the oven and roast for 10 to 15 minutes or until tender and beginning to brown. Remove the sheet pan and add the walnuts. Toss with the maple syrup and half the lemon juice. Return to the oven for 10 additional minutes. Check on the carrots regularly to ensure they do not burn. Remove from the oven and keep warm.

2. **Prepare the chickpeas:** Toss chickpeas with the remaining lemon juice, cayenne powder, and paprika. Taste and season with salt and pepper. Add the arugula and drizzle with the remaining 1 teaspoon extra-virgin olive oil. Toss to combine.

3. **To serve:** Divide the arugula and chickpeas between plates and pile the warm carrots and walnuts on top. Tear the mozzarella into bite-size pieces and arrange on each salad. Drizzle with a touch of extra-virgin olive oil and a pinch of flaky sea salt, if desired. Enjoy!

PLAN 1: WEEK 3

This seven-day recipe plan includes dinner recipes for five days, all of which serve four. To conquer the grocery store in one shopping trip, the next page outlines a detailed grocery list, with items separated by store department. You will also find storage, freezing, and thawing tips to help you plan your week. This plan focuses on the warmth and sweetness of pears prepared with a savory flair and fresh, flavorful herbs such as dill. Pay special attention to these key players (pears, shallots, and fresh dill) throughout the week and be sure to buy the freshest and healthiest of those ingredients that you can find, because you will use them for multiple recipes. Store produce in a bag in the crisper to keep fresh. Note: Look for pears that are firm with few bruises.

THE MENU

MONDAY
Roasted Pear Salad
with Goat Cheese

TUESDAY
Pork Chops with Sautéed Pears

WEDNESDAY
Simple Poached Fish with Great
Northern Beans and Herbs

THURSDAY
Roasted Chicken in Caramelized
Shallot Broth

FRIDAY
Seared Salmon with Warm
Horseradish Potato Salad

PLAN 1: WEEK 3
CONQUERING THE GROCERY STORE

FOOD SAFETY GUIDELINES

Buying groceries for the entire week can require some forethought, so be sure to refer to the FDA's storage and freezing guidelines for raw ingredients. All fish, chicken, and steak require twenty-four hours to thaw out in the fridge.

Raw fish, shellfish, chicken, and ground meats: Store in fridge for 1–2 days
Steak and pork (roasts and chops): Store in fridge for 3–5 days
Uncooked, unopened bacon: Store in fridge for 1–2 weeks

PROTEIN
- ☐ 4 thick, bone-in pork chops
- ☐ 4 (4-ounce) cod fillets
- ☐ 8 bone-in, skin-on chicken thighs
- ☐ 4 (4-ounce) skin-on salmon fillets

OIL
- ☐ Cooking oil
- ☐ Extra-virgin olive oil

DAIRY
- ☐ 1 tablespoon butter
- ☐ 4 ounces crumbled goat cheese

STOCK
- ☐ 5 cups low-sodium chicken stock
- ☐ 3 cups low-sodium vegetable stock

FRUITS & VEGETABLES
- ☐ 8 firm Bosc or red d'Anjou pears
- ☐ 16 ounces mesclun greens
- ☐ 8 ounces fresh baby spinach
- ☐ 1 cup fresh parsley, finely chopped
- ☐ 1 cup fresh dill
- ☐ 2 lemons
- ☐ 6 shallots
- ☐ 1 small red onion
- ☐ 3 pounds baby potatoes
- ☐ 2 zucchini

PANTRY & SPICES
- ☐ 2 (14.5-ounce) cans great northern beans
- ☐ ½ cup whole pecans
- ☐ Balsamic vinegar
- ☐ Whole-grain mustard
- ☐ Mayonnaise
- ☐ Capers
- ☐ Prepared horseradish
- ☐ Dark brown sugar
- ☐ Sugar
- ☐ Salt
- ☐ Pepper
- ☐ Crushed red pepper

(Continued on next page)

TIP

To speed up the thawing process, place the frozen protein in a resealable storage bag and push out the air before sealing the bag. Place the bag in a bowl and run cold water over the bag. Fill the bowl with water and use a heavy jar (such as peanut butter) to keep the bag submerged below the water. Replace the water every ten minutes with more cold water. Alternatively, allow the water to run at a very slow rate. This will take anywhere from thirty minutes to an hour. Note: To keep bacteria from forming, the water must be at 40°F. If using standing water, do not allow the water to reach room temperature.

Roasted Pear Salad with Goat Cheese

Time to Make: 35 minutes

Serves: 4

WHY THIS RECIPE WORKS

This pear salad is a great way to start the week with sweet, aromatic flavors and plenty of contrasting textures, from warm, roasted pears to soft, crumbly goat cheese, and a rich balsamic butter dressing. This recipe allows you to prepare the ingredients in tandem, which is perfect for a quick weeknight dinner.

SUBSTITUTIONS

Pears: Fuji or Gala apples

Mesclun greens: Baby spinach, kale, or arugula

Pecans: Any nut you prefer, such as walnuts or almonds

Goat cheese: Fresh ricotta or a ball of fresh mozzarella

EQUIPMENT & LEFTOVERS

You'll need: Sheet pan, small saucepan, whisk

Leftovers: Keep all ingredients separate in the fridge if intending to keep leftovers

INGREDIENTS

4 firm Bosc or red d'Anjou pears, trimmed, cored, and sliced into thick wedges

2 tablespoons extra-virgin olive oil, divided

Salt and pepper to taste

½ cup whole pecans

½ cup balsamic vinegar

1 tablespoon butter

16 ounces mesclun greens

1 lemon, juice

4 ounces crumbled goat cheese

(Continued on page 39)

METHOD

1. **Prepare the pears:** Preheat oven to 375°F. Arrange sliced pears on a sheet pan and drizzle with 1 tablespoon of extra-virgin olive oil. Season with salt and pepper and transfer to the oven for 20 minutes or until well-browned. Turn the pears once halfway through cooking. Remove from the oven and add pecans to the pears. Bake for an additional 5 minutes or until the pecans are toasty and slightly darker in color. Be careful not to burn the pecans. Remove from the oven and set aside.

2. **Prepare the balsamic reduction:** As the pears cook, pour the ½ cup balsamic vinegar into a small saucepan. Bring to a boil and then reduce heat and simmer, stirring regularly, for about 10 minutes, until the vinegar is reduced by about half. Taste and season with a sprinkle of salt. Whisk in the butter until melted and emulsified. Turn off the heat and set aside.

3. **Prepare the greens:** Toss mesclun greens with the lemon juice and remaining 1 tablespoon extra-virgin olive oil. Season with a light sprinkle of salt and pepper.

4. **To serve:** Divide the dressed greens between plates and arrange the warm pears and pecans on top. Sprinkle with goat cheese and drizzle the balsamic reduction on top. Enjoy!

Pork Chops with Sautéed Pears

Time to Make: 45 minutes

Serves: 4

WHY THIS RECIPE WORKS

This recipe is sweet and savory with a sauce that pairs perfectly with thick, bone-in pork chops. Best of all, it only requires one oven-safe skillet, which makes cleanup a breeze.

SUBSTITUTIONS

Pork chops: Chicken breasts or thighs (adjust cook time, as needed), or pressed, extra-firm tofu cut into thick slices

Pears: Fuji or Gala apples

EQUIPMENT & LEFTOVERS

You'll need: Paper towel and a large oven-safe skillet or braising pan

Leftovers: Store leftovers in the fridge for 3–4 days

INGREDIENTS

1 cup low-sodium chicken stock

2 tablespoons whole-grain mustard

1 heaping tablespoon dark brown sugar

1 tablespoon cooking oil

4 thick, bone-in pork chops

4 firm Bosc or red d'Anjou pears, trimmed, cored, and cut into wedges

2 shallots, peeled and cut into wedges

Salt and pepper to taste

8 ounces fresh baby spinach

METHOD

1. **Prepare sauce:** In a bowl, prepare the sauce by whisking together the chicken stock, mustard, and brown sugar.

2. **Fry the pork chops:** Preheat oven to 400°F. Heat 1 tablespoon oil in a large oven-safe skillet over medium-high heat until very hot. Add the pork chops and cook without moving for 5 minutes until well-browned. Flip and cook an additional 5 minutes until golden-brown. Do not overcrowd the pan; cook in batches if needed. Transfer the pork chops to a plate.

3. **Cook the pears:** Add the pears and shallots to skillet and cook for 1 to 2 minutes per side until the pears are golden brown all over. Season lightly with salt and pepper to taste. Pour the sauce over the pears and toss gently to coat. Turn off the heat and nestle the pork chops in between the pears.

4. **Bake:** Transfer the skillet or braising pot to the oven and bake for about 15 minutes or until an instant-read thermometer reaches 140–145°F at the thickest part of the chop. Note: Cooking time will vary depending on the thickness of the chop; begin checking the internal temperature after 10 minutes in the oven.

5. **Finish the dish:** Carefully remove the skillet from the oven and transfer the pork chops to a plate to rest for 5 minutes. Meanwhile, carefully stir the spinach into the pears until wilted. If necessary, put the skillet on low heat on the stove, but the skillet should be warm enough that the spinach wilts with no additional heat. Taste and season to your preference with salt and pepper.

6. **To serve:** Divide the pears and spinach between plates and place a pork chop on top. Spoon more sauce over the entire dish. Enjoy!

Simple Poached Fish with Great Northern Beans and Herbs

Time to Make: 30 minutes

Serves: 4

WHY THIS RECIPE WORKS

This is the best Wednesday-night meal because it comes together in just under thirty minutes but is still packed with flavor and brightness thanks to fresh herbs and plenty of lemon.

SUBSTITUTIONS

Cod: Sole, haddock, or halibut

Fresh dill: Fresh tarragon or thyme

EQUIPMENT & LEFTOVERS

You'll need: A wide pot with a lid, foil, zester

Leftovers: Store leftovers in the fridge up to 3 days

INGREDIENTS

1 tablespoon cooking oil

1 shallot, peeled and minced

3 cups low-sodium vegetable stock

Salt, pepper, and crushed red pepper to taste

2 (14.5-ounce) cans great northern beans, drained and rinsed

4 (4-ounce) cod fillets

1 cup fresh parsley, finely chopped

½ cup fresh dill, roughly chopped, a pinch reserved for garnish

1 lemon, juice and zest, a pinch of zest reserved for garnish

Extra-virgin olive oil, optional, for serving

METHOD

1. **Cook the shallot:** In a wide pot, heat 1 tablespoon of cooking oil over medium-high heat. Add the minced shallot and cook, stirring frequently, for 2 to 3 minutes or until beginning to soften and brown.

2. **Prepare the broth:** Add the vegetable stock to the shallot and turn the heat to high. Bring to a low boil and cook for 4 to 5 minutes to allow the flavors to meld. Taste and season with salt, pepper, and crushed red pepper. Stir in beans and reduce heat to low to gently simmer. Add the fish, cover the pot, and poach for 5 to 8 minutes or until the fish is cooked through and completely opaque but not overcooked. Using a slotted spoon, carefully remove the fish from the broth and transfer to a plate and cover with foil.

3. **Finish the broth:** Stir the parsley, dill, lemon juice, and lemon zest into the beans and broth. Cook for 3 to 4 minutes to allow the flavors to meld. Taste and season according to your taste.

4. **To serve:** Ladle the beans and broth into bowls and gently place a piece of fish on top of each bowl. Sprinkle the reserved dill and lemon zest over the fish and drizzle with extra-virgin olive oil, if desired. Enjoy!

Roasted Chicken in Caramelized Shallot Broth

Time to Make: 40 minutes

Serves: 4

WHY THIS RECIPE WORKS

Caramelizing the shallots will add a depth of flavor to ordinary store-bought stock. Ladling that flavor-packed broth over crispy chicken thighs and roasted vegetables? You're on another culinary level.

SUBSTITUTIONS

Chicken thighs: Chicken breasts or, for a vegetarian option, roasted eggplant or butternut squash (cook times will vary)

EQUIPMENT & LEFTOVERS

You'll need: A deep skillet, baking sheet, meat thermometer

Leftovers: Store the broth separately from the chicken and roasted vegetables for 3–4 days in the fridge

INGREDIENTS

1 pound baby potatoes, scrubbed and quartered

2 zucchini, trimmed and diced

2 tablespoons cooking oil, divided

Salt and pepper to taste

8 bone-in, skin-on chicken thighs

3 shallots, peeled and quartered

1 teaspoon sugar

4 cups low-sodium chicken stock

METHOD

1. **Prepare the potatoes and zucchini:** Toss the potatoes and zucchini on a baking sheet with 1 tablespoon of oil and season all over with salt and pepper.

2. **Prepare the chicken:** Preheat oven to 425°F. In a deep skillet, heat the remaining 1 tablespoon oil over medium-high. Add the chicken thighs skin-side down, in batches if necessary, and cook the chicken for about 5 minutes until browned and crispy. As the chicken thighs brown, transfer them to the baking sheet, skin-side up, and nestle into the potatoes and zucchini. Once all the chicken thighs are browned and are arranged on the baking sheet, transfer to the oven for 25 to 30 minutes or until an instant-read thermometer reaches 165°F on the chicken and potatoes are fork-tender and browned.

3. **Prepare the caramelized shallot broth:** As the chicken is baking, drain off all but 1 tablespoon of fat from the skillet and return to medium-low heat. Add the shallots and sugar and cook for 10 to 12 minutes, stirring often, until browned. Adjust the heat as necessary to keep the shallots from burning. Pour in chicken stock and scrape up any browned bits stuck to the bottom. Turn heat to high and bring to a boil. Boil for 5 to 7 minutes to allow the broth to reduce slightly. Turn heat to low and simmer until the chicken is finished baking.

4. **To serve:** Divide the roasted potatoes and zucchini between shallow bowls. Ladle the caramelized shallot broth over the vegetables and place a chicken thigh on each dish. Serve with the remaining chicken thighs at the table. Enjoy!

Seared Salmon with Warm Horseradish Potato Salad

Time to Make: 30 minutes

Serves: 4

WHY THIS RECIPE WORKS

This simple dinner of salmon fillets with a warm potato salad is so easy to prepare and allows you to use up any leftover dill you might have hanging out in your fridge. Horseradish and dill work perfectly together to cut through the fattiness of the salmon.

SUBSTITUTIONS

Salmon: Trout fillets or a firm whitefish (such as cod or haddock)

EQUIPMENT & LEFTOVERS

You'll need: Paper towel, large pot, medium skillet

Leftovers: Store the salmon and potatoes separately in the fridge for up to 3 days

INGREDIENTS

2 pounds baby potatoes, halved

4 tablespoons mayonnaise

2½ ounces capers, drained and rinsed

2 tablespoons prepared horseradish plus more to taste

1 small red onion, peeled and thinly sliced

Salt and pepper to taste

½ cup fresh dill, roughly chopped, a pinch reserved for garnish

4 (4-ounce) skin-on salmon fillets

1 tablespoon cooking oil

METHOD

1. **Cook the potatoes:** Cover the potatoes with salted water in a large pot. Bring to a boil and cook for 15 to 20 minutes until fork tender. Drain and then transfer the potatoes back to the same pot and cook over medium heat for 1 to 2 minutes to cook off the excess water.

2. **Prepare the dressing:** While the potatoes are cooking, in a large bowl combine the mayonnaise, capers, horseradish, and thinly sliced onion and toss to combine. Season with salt and pepper. Taste and add more horseradish if a zingier dressing is desired. Set aside.

3. **Finish the salad:** Right before adding the cooked potatoes to the salad, add the chopped dill to the sauce and toss to combine. Add potatoes and gently toss to coat, being careful not to overly mash the potatoes. Taste and season according to your preferences. Keep warm.

4. **Prepare the salmon:** Pat the salmon dry and season all over with salt and pepper. In a medium skillet, heat the cooking oil over medium-high until very hot. Add the salmon, skin-side down, using your spatula to press the fillet into the pan to ensure the skin has good contact with the skillet. Cook the fillets for 5 minutes or until the skin is very crispy and browned. Gently flip and cook an additional 2 to 3 minutes or until the salmon is cooked to your desired internal temperature, 120°F for medium-rare, and 130°F for medium. Remove from heat.

5. **To serve:** Divide the potato salad between plates and gently place a salmon fillet on top. Sprinkle with the reserved chopped dill. Enjoy!

PLAN 1: WEEK 4

This seven-day recipe plan includes dinner recipes for five days, all of which serve four. To conquer the grocery store in one shopping trip, the next page outlines a detailed grocery list, with items separated by store department. You will also find storage, freezing, and thawing tips to help you plan your week. This plan relies on warm, herby flavors paired with earthy root vegetables for dinner recipes that are easy to prepare but still maintain complex flavor profiles. Pay special attention to the key players (fresh chives, watercress, and yellow onions) throughout the week and be sure to buy the freshest and healthiest of those ingredients that you can find, because you will use them for multiple recipes. Store produce in a bag in the crisper to keep fresh. Note: If your store doesn't sell watercress, simply replace it with your favorite tender green.

THE MENU

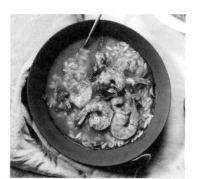

MONDAY
Shrimp and Orzo in a Simple
Tomato Broth

TUESDAY
Twenty-Minute Chicken and Rice

WEDNESDAY
Penne with Turkey Bacon and
Brussels Sprouts

THURSDAY
Seared Pork Tenderloin Salad with
Roasted Carrots and Fresh Mozzarella

FRIDAY
Maple-Sage Roasted Sausage with
Root Vegetables

PLAN 1: WEEK 4
CONQUERING THE GROCERY STORE

FOOD SAFETY GUIDELINES

Buying groceries for the entire week can require some forethought, so be sure to refer to the FDA's storage and freezing guidelines for raw ingredients. All fish, chicken, and steak require twenty-four hours to thaw out in the fridge.

Raw fish, shellfish, chicken, and ground meats: Store in fridge for 1–2 days
Steak and pork (roasts and chops): Store in fridge for 3–5 days
Uncooked, unopened bacon: Store in fridge for 1–2 weeks

PROTEIN
- ☐ 1 pound shrimp, peeled and deveined, tails left on or off depending on preference
- ☐ 1 pound ground chicken
- ☐ 12 ounces turkey bacon, cut into lardons
- ☐ 4 Italian sausages
- ☐ 1 pound pork tenderloin

GRAIN
- ☐ 2 cups dry whole-wheat orzo
- ☐ 16 ounces dry penne
- ☐ 1 cup uncooked white rice

OIL
- ☐ Cooking oil
- ☐ Extra-virgin olive oil

DAIRY
- ☐ 1 tablespoon butter
- ☐ ½ cup heavy cream, optional
- ☐ 1 (8-ounce) ball of fresh mozzarella
- ☐ 2 tablespoons butter

STOCK
- ☐ 4 cups low-sodium vegetable stock
- ☐ 2¾ cups low-sodium chicken stock

FRUITS & VEGETABLES
- ☐ 3 yellow onions
- ☐ 10 cloves garlic
- ☐ 2 sweet potatoes
- ☐ 4 Yukon Gold potatoes
- ☐ 1 lemon
- ☐ ¼ cup fresh parsley
- ☐ 8 ounces cremini mushrooms
- ☐ 1 pint Campari tomatoes
- ☐ 2 tomatoes
- ☐ 8 ounces fresh or frozen green peas
- ☐ 1 ounce fresh chives
- ☐ 1 ounce fresh mint leaves
- ☐ ½ ounce sage leaves
- ☐ 8 ounces Brussels sprouts
- ☐ 1 pound carrots
- ☐ 10 ounces arugula
- ☐ 5 ounces fresh watercress

(Continued on next page)

PANTRY & SPICES

- ☐ Whole-grain or Dijon mustard
- ☐ Tomato paste
- ☐ Maple syrup
- ☐ Sugar
- ☐ Garlic powder
- ☐ Salt
- ☐ Pepper
- ☐ Crushed red pepper

TIP

To speed up the thawing process, place the frozen protein in a resealable storage bag and push out the air before sealing the bag. Place the bag in a bowl and run cold water over the bag. Fill the bowl with water and use a heavy jar (such as peanut butter) to keep the bag submerged below the water. Replace the water every ten minutes with more cold water. Alternatively, allow the water to run at a very slow rate. This will take anywhere from thirty minutes to an hour. Note: To keep bacteria from forming, the water must be at 40°F. If using standing water, do not allow the water to reach room temperature.

Shrimp and Orzo in a Simple Tomato Broth

Time to Make: 40 minutes

Serves: 4

WHY THIS RECIPE WORKS

This broth is flavorful thanks not only to sautéed aromatics but also to a very special, very important ingredient: tomato paste. An often-underused pantry staple, tomato paste is pure, concentrated flavor. This recipe takes the flavor up another level simply by adding the tomato paste after the aromatics have had time to brown a bit. Sautéing tomato paste causes it to deepen in color and, more importantly, in flavor. It only takes a few minutes, so be careful not to burn the paste and to adjust the heat as necessary.

SUBSTITUTIONS

Shrimp: Cod, haddock, or another firm whitefish

EQUIPMENT & LEFTOVERS

You'll need: Paper towel, 2 small pots, colander, 1 medium skillet

Leftovers: Combine the ingredients into one bowl and store in the fridge for up to 3 days

INGREDIENTS

2 cups dry whole-wheat orzo

1 teaspoon extra-virgin olive oil

2 tablespoons cooking oil, divided

1 yellow onion, peeled and minced

6 cloves garlic, peeled and minced

Crushed red pepper to taste

3 tablespoons tomato paste

4 cups low-sodium vegetable stock

1 cup water

Pinch sugar, to taste

1 pound shrimp, peeled and deveined, tails left on or off depending on preference

Salt and pepper to taste

¼ cup fresh parsley, roughly chopped

(Continued on page 53)

METHOD

1. **Cook the orzo:** Bring a pot of salted water to a boil and cook the orzo for 7 to 8 minutes until al dente. Do not overcook the orzo. Transfer the orzo to a bowl and toss with 1 teaspoon extra-virgin olive oil. Set aside.

2. **Prepare the broth:** While the orzo is cooking, in a saucepan heat 1 tablespoon cooking oil over medium heat. Once hot, add the minced yellow onion, garlic, and a pinch of crushed red pepper. Cook for 45 seconds until fragrant. Add the tomato paste and stir frequently, lightly mashing the paste into the vegetables in the pot. Cook for 2 to 3 minutes until the paste begins to deepen in color. Add vegetable stock and stir into the paste until smooth. Add 1 cup water and bring to a boil. Add a pinch of sugar and reduce heat, cover, and cook for 20 minutes to allow the flavors to meld. After 20 minutes, taste the broth and season according to your preference. Cover and keep warm over very low heat, stirring occasionally.

3. **Cook the shrimp:** Once the broth is ready to serve, pat the shrimp dry and season with salt and pepper. Heat the remaining 1 tablespoon of cooking oil in a skillet over medium-high. Add shrimp and cook in an even layer without moving for 90 seconds. Flip and cook an additional 90 seconds or until the shrimp are opaque and cooked through. Transfer to a plate and keep warm. Note: Do not overcrowd skillet; cook the shrimp in batches if necessary.

4. **To serve:** Divide the orzo between bowls. Ladle the tomato broth over each bowl of orzo and arrange the cooked shrimp on top. Garnish with fresh parsley. Enjoy!

Twenty-Minute Chicken and Rice

Time to Make: 20 minutes

Serves: 4

WHY THIS RECIPE WORKS

Who doesn't love a dinner that's done in less than thirty minutes? This easy chicken and rice recipe only requires a handful of ingredients but still delivers on flavor.

SUBSTITUTIONS

White rice: Brown or wild rice, cooking time will vary

Ground chicken: Ground turkey, ground pork, or meat-free crumbles

Cremini mushroom: Any mushroom variety

Campari tomatoes: Cherry tomatoes or 1 (14.5-ounce) can diced tomatoes

Green peas: Diced carrots or edamame

EQUIPMENT & LEFTOVERS

You'll need: Small pot with a lid, skillet

Leftovers: Store leftovers in the fridge for 3–4 days

INGREDIENTS

1 cup uncooked white rice

2 cups water

1 teaspoon extra-virgin olive oil

Salt to taste

1 tablespoon cooking oil, more if needed

1 pound ground chicken

Pepper to taste

8 ounces cremini mushrooms, cleaned and thinly sliced

1 pint Campari tomatoes, halved

1 tablespoon butter

1¾ cups low-sodium chicken stock

8 ounces fresh or frozen, thawed green peas

2 teaspoons of garlic powder

½ ounce fresh chives, finely chopped, a pinch reserved for garnish

2 teaspoons crushed red pepper or more or less to taste

METHOD

1. **Cook the rice:** Combine rice and 2 cups water, 1 teaspoon extra-virgin olive oil, and a sprinkle of salt in a small pot over medium-high heat. Bring to a boil, reduce heat, stir once, and cover. Simmer the rice for 15 minutes and then turn off the heat.

2. **Fry the chicken:** While the rice is cooking, heat the cooking oil in a skillet over medium-high heat. Add the ground chicken, season with salt and pepper, and cook for 7 to 8 minutes or until chicken is cooked through. Transfer to a bowl.

3. **Cook the vegetables:** Add the mushrooms and tomatoes and cook for 3 to 5 minutes over medium-high until they just begin to soften and turn golden brown. Add the butter. Once melted, pour in the chicken stock and bring to a boil. Add peas and cooked chicken and season with salt, pepper, garlic powder, chives, and crushed red pepper. Boil everything for 3 to 5 minutes to allow the sauce to reduce slightly. Turn off the heat.

4. **To serve:** Divide the cooked rice between shallow bowls and ladle the ground chicken and vegetables on top. Garnish with a sprinkle of chives, if desired. Enjoy!

Penne with Turkey Bacon and Brussels Sprouts

Time to Make: 30 minutes

Serves: 4

WHY THIS RECIPE WORKS

So few ingredients to prepare, but so much big flavor! Adding the Brussels sprouts to the pot of boiling water just a minute or two before the pasta is al dente will save you a pot and helps keep the sprouts from overcooking.

SUBSTITUTIONS

Penne: Any tubular pasta such as rigatoni or ziti

Turkey bacon: Pork bacon or loose Italian sausage

Heavy cream: Whole milk, or omit if a lighter recipe is desired

EQUIPMENT & LEFTOVERS

You'll need: Large pot, colander, large skillet

Leftovers: Store leftovers in the fridge for 3–4 days

INGREDIENTS

12 ounces turkey bacon, cut into lardons

1 yellow onion, peeled and small-diced

4 cloves garlic, peeled and minced

1 teaspoon crushed red pepper

2 tomatoes, trimmed, cored, and diced

Salt and pepper to taste

16 ounces dry penne

8 ounces Brussels sprouts, trimmed and halved

½ cup heavy cream, optional

Extra-virgin olive oil, optional, for serving

METHOD

1. **Bring a large pot of salted water to a boil.**

2. **Cook bacon and aromatics:** Fry turkey bacon in large skillet until crispy, about 5 to 7 minutes. Using a slotted spoon, remove bacon and transfer to a bowl. Drain off all but 1 tablespoon of fat in the skillet. Add onion and fry until golden brown and very soft, about 6 to 7 minutes over medium heat. Add garlic, crushed red pepper, and tomatoes and continue to cook, stirring regularly, for 10 to 12 minutes or until very soft. Season to taste with salt and pepper.

3. **Prepare the pasta:** As the tomatoes cook with the aromatics, add the penne to the boiling water and set a timer according to package instructions. Two minutes before the penne is al dente, reserve ½ cup cooking water, then add Brussels sprouts to the water. Boil for only 2 minutes longer. Once the sprouts are bright green, drain the pasta and sprouts into a colander and rinse under cold water. Set aside.

4. **Finish the sauce:** If using heavy cream, add it to the reserved cooking water and stir to combine. Pour into the skillet of sauce and bring to a low boil. Reduce heat and simmer until thickened, about 5 minutes. Taste and season to your preference. Add half the cooked bacon and then the pasta and Brussels sprouts and toss to coat. Cook an additional minute or two to fully coat the pasta with sauce.

5. **To serve:** Divide pasta between bowls and sprinkle each bowl with reserved bacon. Drizzle with a touch of extra-virgin olive oil, if desired. Enjoy!

Seared Pork Tenderloin Salad with Roasted Carrots and Fresh Mozzarella

Time to Make: 30 minutes

Serves: 4

WHY THIS RECIPE WORKS

This pork tenderloin salad is ultra-versatile. Although the lemon-mint dressing is stunning, you can replace the mint with any seasonal herbs, such as thyme, basil, parsley, or chives.

SUBSTITUTIONS

Pork tenderloin: Boneless pork chops, chicken thighs or breasts, or cubed butternut squash for a vegetarian version

Arugula: Watercress, baby spinach, or mesclun greens

Mozzarella: Fresh ricotta or crumbled goat cheese

Mint: Fresh thyme, basil, parsley, or chives

EQUIPMENT & LEFTOVERS

You'll need: Paper towel, sheet pan, oven-safe skillet, zester, meat thermometer

Leftovers: Keep salad ingredients separate and store in the fridge for 3–4 days

INGREDIENTS

1 pound carrots, scrubbed, trimmed, and halved
  lengthwise
½ cup extra-virgin olive oil, divided
Salt and pepper to taste
2 tablespoons cooking oil
1 pound pork tenderloin
1 lemon, juice and zest
2 tablespoons granulated sugar
2 tablespoons whole-grain or Dijon mustard
1 ounce fresh mint leaves
10 ounces arugula
1 (8-ounce) ball of fresh mozzarella

METHOD

1. **Cook the carrots:** Preheat oven to 400°F. On a sheet pan, toss the prepared carrots in 2 tablespoons of extra-virgin olive oil and season with salt and pepper. Transfer to the oven and cook for about 25 to 30 minutes until browned on the edges and cooked through, flipping once halfway through roasting.

2. **Cook pork:** In an oven-safe skillet, heat 2 tablespoons cooking oil over medium-high until very hot. Add the pork tenderloin and cook for 3 to 4 minutes per side until well seared all over. Transfer to the oven for 12 to 15 minutes or until instant-read thermometer reaches 140–145°F for medium rare. Remove from the oven and rest for 5 minutes before slicing.

3. **Prepare the lemon-mint dressing:** As the pork and carrots are roasting, combine the lemon juice and zest with the remaining extra-virgin olive oil, sugar, and mustard. Whisk until smooth. Gently fold in the mint leaves. Taste and season with salt and pepper and set aside.

4. **To serve:** Divide the arugula between bowls and drizzle lightly with half the lemon-mint dressing. Arrange the sliced pork tenderloin and roasted carrots on top and arrange the torn mozzarella around the dish. Drizzle the remaining dressing over the entire plate. Enjoy!

Maple-Sage Roasted Sausage with Root Vegetables

Time to Make: 30 minutes

Serves: 4

WHY THIS RECIPE WORKS

This roasted sausage meal is easy to prepare with a handful of ingredients that are all super customizable. Simply prepare the roasted sausage and potatoes with a bit of stock, herbs, butter, and maple syrup for a final product that tastes like heaven!

SUBSTITUTIONS

Sausage: Vegetarian, pork, or chicken sausage

Sweet potatoes and Yukon Gold potatoes: Mix and match your favorite root vegetables such as parsnips, celery root, turnips, or carrots, or use butternut or acorn squash

Watercress: Arugula, baby spinach, or baby kale

Fresh chives: Fresh sage or fresh thyme

Maple syrup: Honey or brown sugar

EQUIPMENT & LEFTOVERS

You'll need: Paper towel, sheet pan, oven-safe skillet, meat thermometer

Leftovers: Keep salad ingredients separate and store in the fridge for 3–4 days

INGREDIENTS

1 tablespoon cooking oil plus more if necessary

2 sweet potatoes, scrubbed and medium-diced

4 Yukon Gold potatoes, scrubbed and medium-diced

1 yellow onion, peeled and thinly sliced

Salt and pepper to taste

½ teaspoon garlic powder

4 Italian sausages

2 tablespoons butter

2 tablespoons maple syrup

½ ounce fresh chives, minced

½ ounce sage leaves, sliced

1 cup low-sodium chicken stock

5 ounces fresh watercress

1 teaspoon extra-virgin olive oil

Pinch of sea salt

(Continued on next page)

METHOD

1. **Fry the potatoes:** Heat the oil in a large oven-safe skillet over medium-high until very hot. Add sweet potatoes and Yukon Gold potatoes and cook for 5 minutes or until beginning to brown. Add the onion and cook for an additional 5 to 6 minutes or until just beginning to soften and brown. Season all over with salt, pepper, and garlic powder. The potatoes should not be cooked completely through. Once cooked, scoop the potatoes out and transfer to a bowl.

2. **Fry the sausages:** If the skillet seems dry, add a bit more cooking oil and turn the heat back to medium-high. Add sausages and cook for 2 minutes per side or until well-browned all over. Remove and transfer to a plate.

3. **Prepare the sauce:** Add the butter to the skillet and stir until melted and frothy over medium heat. Next, add maple syrup, chives, and sliced sage and cook for 30 seconds until fragrant. Finally, add chicken stock and bring to a boil. Boil for 3 to 5 minutes and then return the potatoes and onions to the pan. Arrange the sausages on top and transfer to the oven. Bake for 20 minutes or until the sausages reach 160°F internal temperature. Remove from heat.

4. **Dress the watercress:** In a bowl, combine the watercress with 1 teaspoon of extra-virgin olive oil and a pinch of sea salt and toss to combine.

5. **To serve:** Divide the potatoes between bowls and arrange the dressed greens on top. Serve with a sausage on top of each dish. Enjoy!

PLAN 2: WEEK 1

This seven-day recipe plan includes dinner recipes for five days, all of which serve four. To conquer the grocery store in one shopping trip, the next page outlines a detailed grocery list, with items separated by store department. You will also find storage, freezing, and thawing tips to help you plan your week. This plan's flavor profile is warm and earthy and uses fresh herbs and aromatics in simple ways for the most impactful flavors. Pay special attention to the key players (sage, fresh mushrooms, and fresh parsley) throughout the week and be sure to buy the freshest and healthiest of those ingredients that you can find, because you will use them for multiple recipes. Store produce in a bag in the crisper to keep fresh. Note: Shiitake stems are too fibrous to eat, but they do impart an earthy flavor on broth, so be sure to save the stems in the crisper for the Poached Fish Udon recipe (page 71).

THE MENU

MONDAY
Mushroom Pasta with Sage and Butter

TUESDAY
Vegan Mushroom Barley Skillet

WEDNESDAY
Poached Fish Udon

THURSDAY
Braised Chicken with Leeks and Tomatoes

FRIDAY
Vegan Soba Salad

CONQUERING THE GROCERY STORE

FOOD SAFETY GUIDELINES

Buying groceries for the entire week can require some forethought, so be sure to refer to the FDA's storage and freezing guidelines for raw ingredients. All fish, chicken, and steak require twenty-four hours to thaw out in the fridge.

Raw fish, shellfish, chicken, and ground meats: Store in fridge for 1–2 days
Steak and pork (roasts and chops): Store in fridge for 3–5 days
Uncooked, unopened bacon: Store in fridge for 1–2 weeks

PROTEIN

- ☐ 4 (4-ounce) cod fillets
- ☐ 4 chicken leg quarters (thigh and drumstick)

GRAIN

- ☐ 16-ounces dry tubular pasta
- ☐ 1 cup pearled barley
- ☐ 1 cup pearl couscous
- ☐ 16 ounces udon noodles
- ☐ 16 ounces soba noodles

OIL

- ☐ Cooking oil
- ☐ Extra-virgin olive oil

DAIRY

- ☐ 2 tablespoons butter
- ☐ ½ cup heavy cream, optional

STOCK

- ☐ 10½ cups low-sodium vegetable stock
- ☐ 3 cups low-sodium chicken stock

FRUITS & VEGETABLES

- ☐ 1 pound mixed mushrooms
- ☐ 1 pound shiitake mushrooms (with stems)
- ☐ 1 pound Roma tomatoes
- ☐ 2 red bell peppers
- ☐ 2 yellow squash
- ☐ 7½ ounces baby spinach
- ☐ 2 leeks
- ☐ 1 yellow onion
- ☐ ½ ounce fresh sage
- ☐ 1 cup fresh parsley
- ☐ 1 lemon
- ☐ 1 lime
- ☐ 2 heads of garlic

PANTRY & SPICES

- ☐ Soy sauce
- ☐ Sesame oil
- ☐ Dry thyme
- ☐ Dry chives
- ☐ Mustard seeds
- ☐ Garlic powder
- ☐ Seasoned rice vinegar
- ☐ Sesame seeds
- ☐ Brown sugar
- ☐ Salt
- ☐ Pepper
- ☐ Crushed red pepper
- ☐ Sriracha, optional
- ☐ Chili oil, optional

TIP

To speed up the thawing process, place the frozen protein in a resealable storage bag and push out the air before sealing the bag. Place the bag in a bowl and run cold water over the bag. Fill the bowl with water and use a heavy jar (such as peanut butter) to keep the bag submerged below the water. Replace the water every ten minutes with more cold water. Alternatively, allow the water to run at a very slow rate. This will take anywhere from thirty minutes to an hour. Note: To keep bacteria from forming, the water must be at 40°F. If using standing water, do not allow the water to reach room temperature.

Mushroom Pasta with Sage and Butter

Time to Make: 30 minutes

Serves: 4

WHY THIS RECIPE WORKS

This comforting mushroom pasta is the perfect way to start the week. The sauce only requires a handful of ingredients and comes together in just about thirty minutes.

SUBSTITUTIONS

Sage: 2 tablespoons fresh rosemary or 1 teaspoon dry sage or dry rosemary

Shiitake mushrooms: Any mushroom variety

Heavy cream: Sour cream

EQUIPMENT & LEFTOVERS

You'll need: Large pot, wide pot, whisk

Leftovers: Store leftovers in the fridge for up to 3 days

INGREDIENTS

16 ounces dry tubular pasta

1 tablespoon cooking oil plus more if necessary

1 yellow onion, peeled and diced

1 pound shiitake mushrooms, caps thinly sliced and
    stems reserved for later in the week

Salt and pepper to taste

2 tablespoons butter

½ ounce fresh sage

3 cups vegetable stock

½ cup sour cream or heavy cream, optional

Extra-virgin olive oil, optional, for serving

¼ cup Parmesan cheese, optional, for serving

METHOD

1. **Boil the pasta:** Bring a large pot of salted water to a boil. Cook the pasta according to package instructions. Reserve ½ cup cooking water and set aside. Drain the pasta and set aside.

2. **Start the sauce:** Meanwhile, prepare the sauce. Heat 1 tablespoon oil in a wide pot over medium-high until very hot. Add the onion and cook, stirring often, until beginning to brown and soften. Add mushrooms and continue to cook, stirring often, for 8 to 10 additional minutes or until well-browned all over. Season with salt and pepper. Add the butter and cook until melted and frothy. Tear the sage leaves and add to the butter. Pour in the stock and scrape up any browned bits stuck to the bottom. Bring to a boil and then reduce heat and simmer for 20 minutes. Scoop out a couple spoonsful of the sauce into a bowl and add the sour cream or heavy cream. Whisk until smooth and creamy and add the mixture back to the sauce and stir to incorporate. Taste and season to your preferences.

3. **Finish the sauce:** Pour in the reserved pasta cooking water. Add the pasta and toss to coat. Turn off the heat. Taste and season again.

4. **To serve:** Divide the pasta between shallow bowls. Drizzle with extra-virgin olive oil and a sprinkle of grated Parmesan cheese, if desired. Enjoy!

Vegan Mushroom Barley Skillet

Time to Make: 50–55 minutes

Serves: 4

WHY THIS RECIPE WORKS

This vegan mushroom barley skillet is earthy and hearty, but the addition of parsley and lemon juice at the very end of cooking adds the right amount of brightness and acidity to this one-skillet wonder. The mushrooms will release a lot of liquid into the skillet, but be careful to not continue the recipe until the liquid has completely evaporated and the mushrooms have turned golden brown. If you use shiitake mushrooms for this recipe, store the stems in the crisper to use later in the week.

SUBSTITUTIONS

Pearled barley: Brown rice, white rice, or quinoa (cook time may vary)

EQUIPMENT & LEFTOVERS

You'll Need: Large skillet

Leftovers: Store leftovers in the fridge for up to 4 days

INGREDIENTS

1 tablespoon cooking oil plus more if necessary

1 pound mixed mushrooms, trimmed and sliced

Salt and pepper to taste

1 teaspoon dry thyme

1 teaspoon mustard seeds

1 teaspoon dry chives

½ teaspoon garlic powder

1 cup pearled barley

3½ cups low-sodium vegetable stock

10 ounces baby spinach

½ cup fresh parsley leaves, roughly chopped, a pinch reserved for garnish

1 lemon, juice

Extra-virgin olive oil, optional, for serving

METHOD

1. **Cook the mushrooms:** In a large skillet, heat 1 tablespoon oil over medium-high until very hot. Add the sliced mushrooms and cook, stirring often, for 8 to 10 minutes until softened and golden brown. If the skillet seems dry, add a bit more oil. Season the mushrooms with salt, pepper, thyme, mustard seeds, chives, and garlic powder and toss to combine.

2. **Cook the barley:** Add the pearled barley to the skillet and cook for 2 to 3 minutes, stirring regularly. Pour in the vegetable stock and scrape up any browned bits stuck to the bottom. Bring to a boil and then reduce heat and simmer for 35 to 40 minutes or until the barley is tender and the liquid is absorbed. Stir the barley occasionally, and, if it is sticking, add a few splashes of water as necessary. Stir in baby spinach along with a big pinch of chopped parsley and lemon juice. Taste and season with salt and pepper. Remove from heat.

3. **To serve:** Spoon mushrooms and barley into bowls and garnish with the reserved chopped parsley and a drizzle of extra-virgin olive oil, if desired. Enjoy!

Poached Fish Udon

Time to Make: 30 minutes

Serves: 4

WHY THIS RECIPE WORKS

Use up any leftover shiitake stems in the crisper for this flavorful and easy-to-prepare udon recipe.

SUBSTITUTIONS

Cod: Hake, haddock, halibut, or another firm whitefish

Udon noodles: Soba noodles or ramen noodles

EQUIPMENT & LEFTOVERS

You'll Need: Paper towel, wide pot, medium pot

Leftovers: Keep cooked noodles, broth, and fish in separate containers in the fridge for up to 2 days

INGREDIENTS

4 cups low-sodium vegetable stock

2 tablespoons soy sauce

2 teaspoons dry chives plus more for serving

1 tablespoon plus 1 teaspoon sesame oil, divided

1 tablespoon seasoned rice vinegar

Leftover shiitake stems from Mushroom Pasta with Sage and Butter recipe (page 67), scrubbed

16 ounces udon noodles

4 (4-ounce) cod fillets

Salt and pepper to taste

Sesame seeds, optional, for serving

Crushed red pepper flakes, optional, for serving

Chili oil, optional, for serving

METHOD

1. **Start the broth:** In a wide pot, combine vegetable stock, soy sauce, chives, 1 tablespoon sesame oil, and rice vinegar. Add the shiitake stems and bring to a boil. Reduce heat, cover, and simmer for 20 minutes. Taste and season to your preference. Using a slotted spoon, scoop out the shiitake stems and discard.

2. **Prepare the udon noodles:** Prepare the udon noodles according to package instructions in a medium pot. Drain, rinse and drizzle with remaining 1 teaspoon sesame oil. Set aside.

3. **Prepare the cod:** After the broth has simmered, pat the fillets dry and season with salt and pepper. Gently place into the broth and cover. Cook for 6 to 8 minutes or until the cod is opaque and flakes easily. Turn off the heat.

4. **To serve:** Divide the noodles between shallow bowls and place a cod fillet on top of each bowl. Ladle the broth over the fish and noodles. Garnish each dish with a sprinkle of sesame seeds, dry chives, and crushed red pepper, if desired. If more heat is desired, drizzle each bowl with a bit of chili oil. Enjoy!

Braised Chicken with Leeks and Tomatoes

Time to Make: 55 minutes

Serves: 4

WHY THIS RECIPE WORKS

Braised chicken always has a delicate richness to it that pairs perfectly with aromatic leeks and garlic and the acidity of fresh tomatoes.

SUBSTITUTIONS

Leeks: Yellow onions

Fresh Roma tomatoes: 1 (14.5-ounce) can whole peeled tomatoes

EQUIPMENT & LEFTOVERS

You'll need: Paper towel, oven-safe braising pot, medium pot

Leftovers: Store leftover couscous and chicken in separate containers in the fridge for 3–4 days

INGREDIENTS

1 tablespoon cooking oil

4 chicken leg quarters (thigh and drumstick)

1 pound Roma tomatoes, quartered

1 head of garlic, peeled and minced

2 leeks, trimmed, washed, halved, and cut into thin half-moons

4 teaspoons extra-virgin olive oil, divided

Salt and pepper to taste

3 cups low-sodium chicken stock

1 cup pearl couscous

1¼ cup of water

½ cup fresh parsley, roughly chopped

METHOD

1. **Fry the chicken:** Preheat oven to 400°F. Heat 1 tablespoon cooking oil in a large oven-safe braising pot. Add the chicken, skin-side down, and cook for 5 minutes until the skin is crispy and browned. Flip and cook an additional 2 to 3 minutes. Remove and transfer to a plate. Drain off all but 1 tablespoon of chicken fat in the pot.

2. **Prepare the vegetables:** As the chicken is frying, in a bowl combine the tomatoes, garlic, and leeks, drizzle with 2 teaspoons extra-virgin olive oil, and season with salt and pepper.

3. **Prepare the braising liquid:** Add the bowl of tomatoes, leeks, and garlic to the braising pot and cook for 5 minutes over medium heat until they begin to soften. Turn heat to high and cook an additional minute or two. Pour in the stock and scrape up any browned bits stuck to the bottom.

4. **Braise the chicken:** Nestle chicken back into the braising pot and transfer to the oven, uncovered, for 30 to 35 minutes or until an instant-read thermometer reaches 165°F.

5. **Prepare the pearl couscous:** In a medium pot, heat the remaining 2 teaspoons extra-virgin olive oil over medium-high heat. Add the pearl couscous and cook, stirring often, for 3 to 4 minutes or until the couscous turns deep golden brown. Add water and bring to a boil. Reduce heat and cover. Cook for 10 to 12 minutes or until all the liquid is absorbed and the couscous is tender. Season with salt and pepper and stir in chopped parsley. Keep warm.

6. **To serve:** Divide the cooked pearl couscous between shallow bowls. Ladle broth with leeks and tomatoes over the couscous and serve with a chicken leg on top. Enjoy!

Vegan Soba Salad

Time to Make: 30 minutes

Serves: 4

WHY THIS RECIPE WORKS

Only a few ingredients and a couple simple steps stand between you and this delicious soba salad recipe. What makes this recipe so easy is just tossing the chopped vegetables right into the pot of boiling water right before the soba reaches al dente. Everything is then tossed with a simple sauce made with a holy trinity of flavors: garlic, soy, and sesame oil.

SUBSTITUTIONS

Soba noodles: Udon or linguine

Bell peppers and squash: Crisp vegetables of your choice such as sugar snap peas, asparagus, green beans, or carrots

Baby spinach: Arugula or mizuna

EQUIPMENT & LEFTOVERS

You'll need: Large pot, whisk, zester

Leftovers: Store leftovers in the fridge for 3–4 days

INGREDIENTS

16 ounces soba noodles

2 red bell peppers, trimmed, deseeded, and finely chopped

2 yellow squash, trimmed and finely chopped

2 tablespoons sesame oil, divided

Salt and pepper to taste

3 tablespoons soy sauce

1 tablespoon brown sugar

1 tablespoon seasoned rice vinegar

2 cloves garlic, peeled and minced

1 lime, juice and zest

Sriracha, optional to taste

2 teaspoons sesame seeds plus more for serving

5 ounces baby spinach

METHOD

1. **Cook the soba noodles:** Bring a pot of salted water to a boil and prepare the soba noodles according to package instructions. About 2 minutes before the noodles are al dente, add diced bell peppers and squash to the boiling water. Cook for 2 minutes and then drain and rinse with cold water. Transfer the noodles and vegetables to a large bowl and drizzle with 1 tablespoon sesame oil. Season lightly with salt and pepper.

2. **Prepare the sauce:** In a bowl, combine the remaining 1 tablespoon sesame oil, soy sauce, brown sugar, and rice vinegar. Add the garlic and lime juice and zest. Whisk to combine. Taste and season to your preferences. Add sriracha to taste, if desired, along with the sesame seeds, and whisk again until smooth and combined.

3. **Prepare the salad:** Pour half the sauce over the noodles and vegetables and toss to coat.

4. **To serve:** Divide the fresh baby spinach between plates and arrange the soba salad on top. Drizzle each plate with the remaining sauce and sprinkle with more sesame seeds. Enjoy!

PLAN 2: WEEK 2

This 7-day recipe plan includes dinner recipes for 5 days, all of which serve four. To conquer the grocery store in one shopping trip, the next page outlines a detailed grocery list, with items separated by store department. You will also find storage, freezing, and thawing tips to help you plan your week. This plan's flavor profile combines sweet, citrus flavors with warm, savory vegetables and aromatics, like sweet potatoes and thyme. Pay special attention to the key players throughout the week (broccolini, oranges, and sweet potatoes) and be sure to buy the freshest and healthiest of those ingredients that you can find, because you will use them for multiple recipes. Store produce in a bag in the crisper to keep fresh. Note: Choose large, firm sweet potatoes and store them in a cool, dark, and well-ventilated place.

THE MENU

MONDAY
Roasted Pork Tenderloin with Broccolini, Baby Potatoes, and Mustard-Butter Sauce

TUESDAY
Pappardelle with a Creamy Sweet Potato Sauce

WEDNESDAY
Seared Salmon with Orange-Maple Mashed Sweet Potatoes and Citrus Salt

THURSDAY
Roasted Chicken Salad with Mizuna, Broccolini, and Shaved Carrots

FRIDAY
Orange-Thyme Beef Soup with Kale

FOOD SAFETY GUIDELINES

Buying groceries for the entire week can require some forethought, so be sure to refer to the FDA's storage and freezing guidelines for raw ingredients. All fish, chicken, and steak require twenty-four hours to thaw out in the fridge.

Raw fish, shellfish, chicken, and ground meats: Store in fridge for 1–2 days
Steak and pork (roasts and chops): Store in fridge for 3–5 days
Uncooked, unopened bacon: Store in fridge for 1–2 weeks

PROTEIN

- ☐ 1 pound pork tenderloin
- ☐ 4 (6-ounce) skin-on salmon fillets
- ☐ 8 skin-on, bone-in chicken thighs
- ☐ 1 pound ground beef

GRAIN

- ☐ 16 ounces dry whole-wheat pappardelle pasta

OIL

- ☐ Cooking oil
- ☐ Extra-virgin olive oil

DAIRY

- ☐ 6 tablespoons butter
- ☐ ½ cup heavy cream
- ☐ Shredded Parmesan cheese, optional

STOCK

- ☐ 5 cups low-sodium chicken stock

FRUITS & VEGETABLES

- ☐ 2 bunches broccolini
- ☐ 6 sweet potatoes
- ☐ 4 medium carrots
- ☐ 2 red bell peppers
- ☐ 1 yellow onion
- ☐ 16 ounces baby potatoes
- ☐ 10 ounces mizuna leaves
- ☐ 1 bunch lacinato kale
- ☐ 1 red bell pepper
- ☐ 2 shallots
- ☐ 5 cloves garlic
- ☐ ½ cup basil leaves
- ☐ 2 lemons
- ☐ 3 orange
- ☐ 1 cup fresh parsley

(Continued on next page)

PANTRY & SPICES

- ☐ 1 (15-ounce) can cannellini beans
- ☐ 1 (14.5-ounce) can of crushed tomatoes
- ☐ Whole-grain mustard
- ☐ Maple syrup
- ☐ Brown sugar
- ☐ Sugar
- ☐ Onion powder
- ☐ Dry parsley
- ☐ Dry thyme
- ☐ Dry chives
- ☐ Flaky sea salt
- ☐ Salt
- ☐ Pepper
- ☐ Crushed red pepper

TIP

To speed up the thawing process, place the frozen protein in a resealable storage bag and push out the air before sealing the bag. Place the bag in a bowl and run cold water over the bag. Fill the bowl with water and use a heavy jar (such as peanut butter) to keep the bag submerged below the water. Replace the water every ten minutes with more cold water. Alternatively, allow the water to run at a very slow rate. This will take anywhere from thirty minutes to an hour. Note: To keep bacteria from forming, the water must be at 40°F. If using standing water, do not allow the water to reach room temperature.

Roasted Pork Tenderloin with Broccolini, Baby Potatoes, and Mustard-Butter Sauce

Time to Make: 30 minutes

Serves: 4

WHY THIS RECIPE WORKS

This recipe is simple in ingredients but big on flavor. Parboiling potatoes ensures that they will be fork tender right as the pork is finished cooking, so you won't end up with dry, overcooked meat.

SUBSTITUTIONS

Pork tenderloin: Pork chops or boneless skinless chicken breasts (cook time may vary)

Broccolini: Broccoli or cauliflower florets, frozen green peas, sugar snap peas, or asparagus

EQUIPMENT & LEFTOVERS

You'll need: Medium pot with a lid, large oven-safe skillet

Leftovers: Store leftovers in the fridge for 3–4 days

INGREDIENTS

16 ounces baby potatoes, halved lengthwise

1 tablespoon cooking oil

1 pound pork tenderloin

1 lemon, divided

3 tablespoons butter

1 tablespoon whole-grain mustard

1 tablespoon brown sugar

1 bunch broccolini

Salt and pepper to taste

(Continued on page 81)

METHOD

1. **Parboil the potatoes:** Preheat oven to 400°F. Cover potatoes in a medium pot of salted water. Bring to a boil. Cover and cook for about 6 to 8 minutes until softened but not fork-tender. Drain.

2. **Prepare the pork:** Heat 1 tablespoon oil in a large oven-safe skillet over medium-high until very hot. Add the pork tenderloin and cook for 3 to 4 minutes per side.

3. **Prepare sauce:** While pork is frying, cut the ends off the lemon and set aside. Cut the middle of the lemon into 4 rounds. Melt butter in a small bowl. Squeeze the juice from the lemon ends into the butter. Add in mustard and brown sugar and whisk to combine. Taste and season with salt and pepper. Add the parboiled potatoes around the pork tenderloin in the skillet. Pour the sauce over potatoes and pork tenderloin. Arrange the broccolini on top of the potatoes, drizzle the broccolini with a touch of extra-virgin olive oil, and season with salt. Place lemon rounds on top of broccolini. Transfer to the oven for 12 to 15 minutes or until an instant-read thermometer reaches 140–145°F for medium rare. Remove the skillet from the oven and discard the lemon rounds. Transfer the pork tenderloin to a cutting board. Rest for 5 minutes before slicing.

4. **To serve:** Place the pork tenderloin in the middle of a serving platter and arrange the potatoes and broccolini around the pork. Spoon any extra sauce from the skillet over the pork and vegetables. Serve immediately. Enjoy!

Pappardelle with a Creamy Sweet Potato Sauce

Time to Make: 30–40 minutes

Serves: 4

WHY THIS RECIPE WORKS

Sweet potatoes, red bell peppers, and a big pile of aromatics are roasted, pureed, and then combined with a spicy tomato base and topped off with a bit of cream to create the ultimate sauce that is just a bit sweet, fragrant, and spicy. If using a food processor or blender, follow the recipe as written. If using an immersion blender, simply add the roasted vegetables to the tomato base and blend with the immersion blender until smooth and creamy.

SUBSTITUTIONS

Pappardelle: 16 ounces whole-wheat pasta of your choice

EQUIPMENT & LEFTOVERS

You'll need: 2 large pots, baking sheet, food processor (or immersion blender or regular blender)

Leftovers: Store leftovers in the fridge for up to 3–5 days

INGREDIENTS

16 ounces dry whole-wheat pappardelle pasta

2 teaspoons extra-virgin olive oil

2 medium sweet potatoes, peeled and roughly chopped

1 red bell pepper, trimmed, deseeded, and roughly chopped

5 cloves garlic, peeled

2 shallots, peeled and quartered

1 tablespoon cooking oil

Salt and pepper to taste

½ cup basil leaves, divided

1 (14.5-ounce) can of crushed tomatoes

1 teaspoon dry parsley

½ teaspoon onion powder

1 teaspoon crushed red pepper or more or less to taste

Pinch sugar

Shredded Parmesan cheese, optional, for serving

(Continued on next page)

METHOD

1. **Cook the pasta:** Preheat oven to 400°F. Bring a large pot of salted water to a boil and cook the pappardelle according to the pasta instructions. Reserve 2½ cups of the cooking water. Drain the pasta and rinse and drizzle with 2 teaspoons extra-virgin olive oil. Set aside.

2. **Roast the vegetables:** Transfer the sweet potatoes, pepper, garlic, and shallots to a baking sheet and toss with 1 tablespoon cooking oil. Season with salt and pepper and transfer to the oven. Cook for 30 minutes until fork-tender. Transfer the roasted vegetables to a food processor along with 1 cup reserved cooking water and half the basil leaves and puree until smooth. Set aside.

3. **Prepare the tomato base:** While the vegetables are roasting, in a large pot combine the crushed tomatoes with the parsley, onion powder, crushed red pepper, sugar, salt, and pepper. Bring to a boil. Reduce heat and simmer, uncovered, for 20 to 25 minutes. (The tomato base should be done right as you're finishing roasting and pureeing the vegetables.) Pour the vegetable puree into the sauce along with ¾ cup pasta cooking water and then season the sauce according to your preferences. Simmer for 5 additional minutes. If the pasta sauce seems too thick, add the remaining reserved pasta cooking water in small additions until desired consistency is reached. Taste and season again before serving. Add the cooked pasta to the sauce and toss to coat. Cook an additional minute or two to rewarm the pasta.

4. **To serve:** Divide the pasta between bowls and sprinkle with Parmesan cheese, if using, and arrange the remaining basil leaves on top of each dish. Enjoy!

Seared Salmon with Orange-Maple Mashed Sweet Potatoes and Citrus Salt

Time to Make: 30 minutes

Serves: 4

WHY THIS RECIPE WORKS

Call it what you like, seared, crispy, or fried, this fish is best when the skin is ultra-crispy and a little salty. This seared salmon is tasty on its own but paired with fragrant orange-maple mashed sweet potatoes and citrus salt, this easy-to-cook fish is a sweet, salty, citrusy match made in heaven.

SUBSTITUTIONS

Salmon: Arctic char or skin-on trout fillets

Maple syrup: Honey or brown sugar

EQUIPMENT & LEFTOVERS

You'll need: Paper towel, large pot, skillet, zester, electric hand mixer or potato masher

Leftovers: Store leftovers in the fridge for 3–4 days

INGREDIENTS

2 oranges, zested into one bowl and juiced into another

1 teaspoon flaky sea salt

4 large sweet potatoes, peeled and diced

½ cup heavy cream

2 tablespoons maple syrup

3 tablespoons butter

Salt and pepper to taste

2 teaspoons cooking oil

4 (6-ounce) skin-on salmon fillets

(Continued on page 87)

METHOD

1. **Prepare the citrus salt:** In a small bowl, combine half the orange zest with the 1 teaspoon flaky sea salt and lightly mash the zest into the salt. Stir until well incorporated and set aside.

2. **Prepare sweet potatoes:** Cover sweet potatoes with water in a large pot and add salt. Bring to a boil and cook for 20 minutes or until very tender. Drain. Transfer the potatoes to large bowl with the cream, maple syrup, and butter. Add all the orange juice and the remaining orange zest. Using a hand mixer, beat the mashed sweet potatoes until very smooth and creamy. Taste and season with salt and pepper. (Do not overseason, as you will sprinkle citrus salt on each dish.) Set aside and keep warm.

3. **Cook the salmon:** Lightly season the salmon all over with salt and pepper. Heat 2 teaspoons cooking oil in a skillet over medium-high heat. Once very hot and shimmering, add the salmon skin-side down. Cook for 3 to 4 minutes or until the skin is crispy and releases easily from the skillet. Gently flip the salmon and cook an additional 3 to 5 minutes or until the salmon is opaque and cooked to your desired internal temperature. Be careful not to overcook the salmon. Turn off the heat.

4. **To serve:** Divide the mashed sweet potatoes between plates and use the back of your spoon to smooth them out along each plate. Place a salmon fillet, skin-side up, on top of each plate. Sprinkle each dish with a pinch of the citrus salt. Enjoy!

Roasted Chicken with Mizuna, Broccolini, and Shaved Carrots

Time to Make: 40 minutes

Serves: 4

WHY THIS RECIPE WORKS

Mizuna, also called Japanese mustard greens, is a peppery, dark, leafy green with an absolutely delicious flavor. Not quite as spicy as arugula, these greens are versatile and add plenty of flavor to any salad. This mizuna salad with roasted chicken is the perfect balance of peppery greens, bright carrots, and the deep flavors of roasted broccolini along with the succulent, crispy-skinned chicken.

SUBSTITUTIONS

Mizuna: Arugula or baby spinach

Chicken thighs: Pork chops, chicken breasts, or portobello mushroom caps (cook time may vary)

EQUIPMENT & LEFTOVERS

You'll need: Oven-safe skillet, baking sheet, vegetable peeler

Leftovers: Store leftovers in the fridge for 3–4 days

INGREDIENTS

8 skin-on, bone-in chicken thighs

Salt and pepper to taste

2 teaspoons oil

1 bunch broccolini

1 lemon, thinly sliced

10 ounces mizuna leaves

4 medium carrots, trimmed and peeled into wide ribbons

2 teaspoons extra-virgin olive oil plus more for serving

METHOD

1. **Prepare the chicken:** Preheat oven to 425°F. Pat the chicken dry and season all over with salt and pepper and set aside. In an oven-safe skillet, heat 2 teaspoons oil over medium-high heat. Add the chicken, skin-side down, and cook without moving for 5 to 6 minutes or until the chicken skin is crispy and golden brown. Note: Do not overcrowd the skillet; cook in batches if necessary. Flip and transfer to the oven for 30 minutes or until an instant-read thermometer registers 165°F.

2. **Prepare the broccolini:** On a baking sheet, toss the broccolini with a drizzle of extra-virgin olive oil, salt, and pepper. Arrange the lemon slices on top. During the last 10 minutes of the chicken baking, transfer the broccolini to the oven and bake for 10 minutes. Discard the cooked lemon slices.

3. **Prepare the mizuna salad:** Right before serving, toss the mizuna greens with a drizzle of extra-virgin olive oil in a bowl and a sprinkle of salt and pepper.

4. **To serve:** Place chicken thighs on the far side of a shallow bowl and pile the dressed mizuna greens around. Arrange the broccolini and shaved carrots on top. If desired, drizzle a touch of extra-virgin olive oil on top along with another sprinkle of salt and a crack of black pepper. Enjoy!

Orange-Thyme
Beef Soup with Kale

Time to Make: 35–40 minutes

Serves: 4

WHY THIS RECIPE WORKS

Orange and thyme prove to be a formidable duo in this easy-to-prepare, reinvented ground beef soup recipe.

SUBSTITUTIONS

Lacinato kale: Baby spinach or baby kale

Ground beef: Ground pork, chicken, or turkey or replace with an additional can of beans

Cannellini beans: Garbanzo, navy, or great northern beans

EQUIPMENT & LEFTOVERS

You'll Need: Soup pot, vegetable peeler

Leftovers: Store leftovers in the fridge for 3–4 days

INGREDIENTS

1 tablespoon cooking oil

1 pound ground beef

Salt and pepper to taste

1 yellow onion, peeled and diced

2 red bell peppers, trimmed, deseeded, and diced

5 cups low-sodium chicken stock

1 orange, peeled (peel reserved) and juiced

1 (15-ounce) can cannellini beans, drained and rinsed

1 teaspoon dry thyme

1 teaspoon dry chives

Crushed red pepper to taste

1 bunch lacinato kale, thick center rib removed and leaves roughly chopped

1 cup fresh parsley, roughly chopped

METHOD

1. **Brown the beef:** Heat 1 tablespoon oil in a soup pot over medium-high until very hot. Add the ground beef and cook for 5 minutes until well browned all over, breaking the beef up with a wooden spoon as it cooks. Season with salt and pepper. Transfer to a bowl and drain off all but 1 tablespoon of fat from the pot.

2. **Prepare the vegetables:** Add the diced onion and diced peppers in the pot over medium-high. Cook, stirring regularly until softened and beginning to brown all over, about 5 minutes. Season with salt and pepper.

3. **Prepare the soup:** Pour in the chicken stock and add the orange peels and orange juice. Scrape up any browned bits stuck to the bottom. Bring to a boil. Reduce heat and simmer. Add cooked beef and cannellini beans to the pot. Season with dry thyme, dry chives, and a sprinkle of crushed red pepper. Season with salt and pepper. Cook for 10 to 15 minutes to allow the flavors to meld. Add chopped kale and roughly chopped fresh parsley and cook until wilted but bright green, about 3 to 5 minutes. Turn off heat.

4. **To serve:** Discard orange peels. Ladle the beef soup into bowls and add a sprinkle of crushed red pepper on top of each bowl of soup, if desired.

PLAN 2: WEEK 3

This seven-day recipe plan includes dinner recipes for five days, all of which serve four. To conquer the grocery store in one shopping trip, the next page outlines a detailed grocery list, with items separated by store department. You will also find storage, freezing, and thawing tips to help you plan your week. Pay special attention to the key players (fresh celery and lemons) throughout the week and be sure to buy the freshest and healthiest of those ingredients that you can find, because you will use them for multiple recipes. Store produce in the crisper to keep fresh. Note: If there are leaves on the celery stalks, don't throw them out! Simply chop them up and sauté the leaves with the stalks.

THE MENU

MONDAY
Chicken with Stewed Peppers

TUESDAY
Lemon-Mint Orzo with Shrimp

WEDNESDAY
Spicy Coconut Curry Soba
with Tofu

THURSDAY
Baked Cod and Sausage with Lemon

FRIDAY
Seared Steak with Mushrooms
and Tomatoes

CONQUERING THE GROCERY STORE

FOOD SAFETY GUIDELINES

Buying groceries for the entire week can require some forethought, so be sure to refer to the FDA's storage and freezing guidelines for raw ingredients. All fish, chicken, and steak require twenty-four hours to thaw out in the fridge.

Raw fish, shellfish, chicken, and ground meats: Store in fridge for 1–2 days
Steak and pork (roasts and chops): Store in fridge for 3–5 days
Uncooked, unopened bacon: Store in fridge for 1–2 weeks

PROTEIN

- ☐ 8 skin-on, bone-in chicken thighs
- ☐ 1 pound shrimp, peeled and deveined (tails left on if desired)
- ☐ 1 pound cod
- ☐ 12 ounces loose hot Italian sausage
- ☐ 1 pound boneless steak (such as skirt, bavette, flank, rib eye, or hanger)
- ☐ 16 ounces extra firm tofu

GRAIN

- ☐ 1 cup uncooked white or brown rice
- ☐ 8 ounces dry orzo
- ☐ 8 ounces soba noodles
- ☐ 1 cup uncooked brown or wild rice

OIL

- ☐ Extra-virgin olive oil
- ☐ Cooking oil

DAIRY

- ☐ 2 tablespoons butter, optional

STOCK

- ☐ 4 cups low-sodium chicken stock
- ☐ 7 cups low-sodium vegetable stock

FRUITS & VEGETABLES

- ☐ 8 ounces fresh shiitake mushrooms
- ☐ 8 ounces fingerling potatoes
- ☐ 8 ounces cremini mushrooms
- ☐ 3 zucchini
- ☐ 3 yellow onions
- ☐ 2 red bell peppers
- ☐ 1 pound mini sweet peppers
- ☐ 2 leeks
- ☐ 3 heads of garlic
- ☐ 1 pound Campari tomatoes
- ☐ 6 stalks celery
- ☐ 3 carrots
- ☐ 6 scallions
- ☐ 1-inch piece of ginger
- ☐ 4 lemons
- ☐ ½ ounce fresh sage
- ☐ ½ ounce fresh mint

(Continued on next page)

PANTRY & SPICES

- ☐ 2 (14.5-ounce) cans crushed tomatoes
- ☐ 1 (5.4-ounce) can coconut cream
- ☐ 2 ounces Thai red curry paste
- ☐ 1¾ ounces pine nuts, optional
- ☐ Sesame oil
- ☐ Sweet paprika
- ☐ Smoked sweet or hot paprika, optional
- ☐ Flour
- ☐ Sugar
- ☐ Brown sugar
- ☐ Black or white sesame seeds
- ☐ Salt
- ☐ Pepper
- ☐ Chili oil, optional

TIP

To speed up the thawing process, place the frozen protein in a resealable storage bag and push out the air before sealing the bag. Place the bag in a bowl and run cold water over the bag. Fill the bowl with water and use a heavy jar (such as peanut butter) to keep the bag submerged below the water. Replace the water every ten minutes with more cold water. Alternatively, allow the water to run at a very slow rate. This will take anywhere from thirty minutes to an hour. Note: To keep bacteria from forming, the water must be at 40°F. If using standing water, do not allow the water to reach room temperature.

Chicken with Stewed Peppers

Time to Make: 50 minutes

Serves: 4

WHY THIS RECIPE WORKS

Although this is not quite a traditional, creamy chicken paprikash, this chicken with stewed peppers is still loaded with paprika and served over simple white rice for a no-fuss meal that comes together quickly. If you can't find small, sweet peppers, simply replace with red, orange, or yellow bell peppers.

SUBSTITUTIONS

Leeks: Yellow onion

Mini sweet peppers: Red, orange, or yellow bell peppers

White rice: Brown rice, wild rice, or quinoa (cook time may vary)

EQUIPMENT & LEFTOVERS

You'll need: Paper towel, medium pot with a lid, large oven-safe wide skillet or braising pot, meat thermometer

Leftovers: Store leftovers in the fridge for 3–4 days

INGREDIENTS

2 cups uncooked white or brown rice, cooking time will vary depending on rice

3½ cups water

1 teaspoon salt plus extra to taste

8 skin-on, bone-in chicken thighs

Pepper to taste

1 tablespoon cooking oil

2 leeks, trimmed, washed, and sliced into half-moons

1 pound mini sweet peppers, trimmed, deseeded, and sliced into rounds

6 cloves garlic, peeled and minced

3 tablespoons sweet paprika

½ tablespoon smoked, sweet, or hot paprika, optional

1 tablespoon flour

2 cups chicken stock

1 (14.5-ounce) can crushed tomatoes

1 big pinch granulated sugar

(Continued on page 97)

METHOD

1. **Prepare the rice:** Combine the rice with 3½ cups water and a teaspoon of salt in a medium pot with a lid. Bring to a boil and stir once. Reduce heat to low, cover, and simmer for 15 to 20 minutes, if using white rice. Turn off the heat and allow to rest, covered, for 5 minutes before fluffing with a fork.

2. **Fry the chicken:** Preheat oven to 425°F. Pat the chicken dry and season all over with salt and pepper. In an oven-safe wide skillet or braising pot, heat 1 tablespoon oil over medium-high until very hot. Add the chicken, skin-side down, and cook for 5 minutes until well-browned and crispy. Flip and cook for 2 to 3 minutes more. Transfer the chicken to a skillet and drain off all but 1 tablespoon of oil in the skillet. Return the skillet to medium heat.

3. **Sauté the aromatics:** Add the leeks and peppers to the skillet and cook, stirring often, for 5 minutes or until beginning to soften and brown. Add garlic and cook for 45 seconds more or until fragrant. Reduce the heat to medium. Sprinkle all the paprika over the vegetables and toss to coat. Next, sprinkle the flour over the vegetables and toss to coat. Cook for 45 seconds or until the paprika begins to deepen in color, but be careful not to burn it. Slowly whisk in the chicken stock and add the crushed tomatoes. Bring to a boil and then reduce heat to low. Add a big pinch of sugar and then taste and season with salt and pepper.

4. **Roast the chicken:** Nestle the chicken into the sauce, then transfer to the oven and roast for 25 to 30 minutes or until an instant-read thermometer reaches 165°F. Remove from heat.

5. **To serve:** Spoon the rice into shallow bowls and ladle the stewed peppers on top. Serve with the cooked crispy chicken thighs. Enjoy!

Lemon-Mint Orzo with Shrimp

Time to Make: 35 minutes

Serves: 4

WHY THIS RECIPE WORKS

This lemon-mint orzo with poached shrimp is so easy to prepare and looks so elegant on the table. The brightness of lemon pairs perfectly with fresh mint, juicy poached shrimp, and tender orzo.

SUBSTITUTIONS

Shrimp: Cod or hake (cook time may vary)

EQUIPMENT & LEFTOVERS

You'll need: Paper towel, medium pot, wide pot, fine-mesh sieve

Leftovers: Store leftovers in the fridge for 3–4 days

INGREDIENTS

2 small lemons

8 ounces dry orzo

2 teaspoons extra-virgin olive oil plus more for serving if desired

Salt and pepper to taste

1 teaspoon cooking oil

3 stalks celery, trimmed and diced

5 cloves garlic, peeled and minced

3 cups vegetable stock

1 pound shrimp, peeled and deveined, tails left on or off depending on preference

1¾ ounces pine nuts, optional

½ ounce fresh mint leaves

METHOD

1. **Prepare the lemons:** Thinly slice 1 lemon into rounds. Using a vegetable peeler, peel the other lemon into wide strips and reserve the peels. Then, juice the lemon into a bowl.

2. **Prepare the orzo:** Bring 2 quarts of salted water to a boil in a medium pot. Pour in the orzo and stir immediately to keep the orzo from clumping. Cook for about 8 minutes or until al dente. Reserve ¼ cup cooking water and set aside. Drain and rinse the orzo and transfer to a bowl. Drizzle with 2 teaspoons extra-virgin olive oil and a sprinkle of salt.

3. **Cook the broth:** In a wide pot, heat 1 teaspoon cooking oil until very hot. Add celery and cook for 3 minutes until bright green and softened. Add garlic and cook for 45 seconds or until fragrant. Add the lemon peels and the vegetable stock and bring to a boil. Season with black pepper and crushed red pepper. Stir in the lemon juice. Reduce heat and simmer for 15 minutes. Taste and season with salt and pepper, if desired. Pour the broth into a bowl through a fine-mesh sieve and discard the solids. Wipe out the pot and transfer the broth along with the reserved cooking water back to the pot over high heat.

4. **Poach the shrimp:** Pat the shrimp dry and season all over with salt and pepper. Once the broth is boiling, turn off the heat and add the

(Continued on next page)

shrimp. Cover and cook until the shrimp are opaque and are cooked through, but not overcooked. Stir the shrimp once or twice to ensure they cook through completely.

5. **Prepare the toasted pine nuts, if using:** Heat a small skillet over medium heat. Add the pine nuts and cook, stirring often, for 30 to 45 seconds until golden brown. Turn off the heat and transfer the pine nuts to a small bowl with a sprinkle of salt.

6. **Finish the orzo:** Tear the mint leaves and toss with the orzo.

7. **To serve:** Divide the orzo between bowls and ladle the hot broth and shrimp over each bowl. Sprinkle with toasted pine nuts, a drizzle of extra-virgin olive oil, and a lemon round, if desired. Enjoy!

Spicy Coconut Curry Soba with Tofu

Time to Make: 35–40 minutes

Serves: 4

WHY THIS RECIPE WORKS

Crispy tofu and a spicy, aromatic curry broth come together with loads of vegetables and soba noodles. Both the coconut cream and brown sugar add sweetness and richness to this healthy dinner option.

SUBSTITUTIONS

Soba noodles: Udon or ramen

Tofu: Cubed boneless, skinless chicken breasts (cook time may vary) or omit, if desired

Vegetables: Mix and match any vegetables you like such as eggplant, squash, broccoli, cauliflower, green beans, or asparagus

EQUIPMENT & LEFTOVERS

You'll need: Paper towels, plates, heavy books, soup pot, and a large pot

Leftovers: Store noodles, soup, and tofu in separate containers in the fridge for up to 3 days

INGREDIENTS

16 ounces extra-firm tofu

3 tablespoons cooking oil, divided

1 yellow onion, peeled and thinly sliced

1-inch piece of ginger, peeled and minced

1 head of garlic, peeled and minced

6 scallions, trimmed and minced, light green and dark green parts kept separate

2 ounces Thai red curry paste

4 cups vegetable stock

1 tablespoon brown sugar

3 carrots, peeled and cut into thin rounds

1 red bell pepper, trimmed, deseeded, and thinly sliced

8 ounces fresh shiitake mushrooms, caps thinly sliced and stems discarded

8 ounces soba noodles

1 tablespoon sesame oil

Salt and pepper to taste

1 teaspoon black or white sesame seeds

1 (5.4-ounce) can coconut cream

Chili oil, optional, for serving

(Continued on page 103)

METHOD

1. **Press the tofu:** Wrap the tofu in paper towels and place between two plates. Stack a few heavy books on the top plate and press the tofu as you prepare the rest of the dish.

2. **Prepare the soup base:** In a soup pot, heat 1 tablespoon cooking oil over medium-high until very hot. Add the onion and cook, stirring often, until browned and beginning to soften. Add ginger, garlic, and white and light green (not dark green) parts of the scallions and cook an additional 45 seconds or until fragrant. Add the curry paste and mash it into the aromatics. Once the aromatics are coated, pour in the vegetable stock and brown sugar and bring to a boil. Add the sliced carrots, red bell pepper, and shiitake mushroom caps to the soup and cook for 25 minutes or until vegetables are tender.

3. **Prepare the soba noodles:** Bring a large pot of water to a boil and cook the soba noodles according to package instructions. Drain and rinse. Drizzle with 1 tablespoon sesame oil and set aside.

4. **Fry the tofu:** Unwrap the tofu and pat it dry once more. Cut the tofu into 2-inch cubes. In a wide skillet, heat the remaining 2 tablespoons cooking oil over medium-high until very hot. Add the tofu and cook without moving for 1 to 2 minutes per side or until golden brown and crispy on both sides. Transfer to a plate and sprinkle with salt, pepper, and sesame seeds.

5. **Finish the soup:** Pour the coconut cream into the soup and stir to combine. Taste the soup and season with salt and pepper to taste.

6. **To serve:** Divide the noodles between shallow bowls and ladle the soup over each bowl. Serve with crispy tofu on top. Garnish each dish with the reserved minced dark scallion greens and chili oil, if desired.

Baked Cod and Sausage with Lemon

Time to Make: 45 minutes

Serves: 4

WHY THIS RECIPE WORKS

One oven-safe skillet and a bit of time is all that's needed for this simple dinner recipe that brings together heat from the sausage, delicate, flaky cod, and brightness from the lemons.

SUBSTITUTIONS

Cod: Hake, tilapia, or shrimp (cook time may vary)

Sausage: Fresh chorizo or omit and season generously with crushed red pepper instead

EQUIPMENT & LEFTOVERS

You'll need: Large oven-safe skillet

Leftovers: Store leftovers in the fridge for 3–4 days

INGREDIENTS

1 pound cod

1 tablespoon cooking oil

1 yellow onion, peeled and diced

3 stalks celery, trimmed and thinly sliced

8 ounces fingerling potatoes, halved if small or
    quartered if large

Salt and pepper to taste

12 ounces loose hot Italian sausage

2 cups chicken stock

2 lemons, one juiced and one thinly sliced

1 (14.5-ounce) can diced tomatoes

2 teaspoons extra-virgin olive oil

METHOD

1. **Preheat oven to 400°F:** Pat the cod dry and keep in the refrigerator until ready to use.

2. **Cook the aromatics:** In a large oven-safe skillet, heat 1 tablespoon cooking oil over medium-high until very hot. Add the onion and celery and cook, stirring often, until beginning to brown and soften, about 4 minutes. Add potatoes and cook for 8 to 10 minutes or until beginning to brown all over. Season with salt and pepper. Transfer the potatoes and aromatics to a bowl and leave the skillet on medium-high heat.

3. **Cook the sausage:** Crumble the sausage into the skillet and cook, stirring often, until browned all over, about 5 to 6 minutes. Add chicken stock, lemon juice, and diced tomatoes and stir to combine. Taste and season with salt and pepper. Add the bowl of potatoes and aromatics to the skillet and toss to combine.

4. **Bake the cod:** Place the cod on top of the dish and season all over with salt and pepper. Arrange the sliced lemon all over the dish and drizzle 2 teaspoons extra-virgin olive oil over the cod. Transfer to the oven and bake for 15 to 20 minutes or until the fish is opaque and flakes easily. If desired, transfer the skillet to the broiler for 2 to 3 minutes to char the lemons a bit.

5. **To serve:** Spoon the potatoes and sausage into shallow bowls and serve with the flaked cod. Enjoy!

Seared Steak with Mushrooms and Tomatoes

Time to Make: 30 minutes

Serves: 4

WHY THIS RECIPE WORKS

Our seared steak with mushrooms and tomatoes looks so lovely plated that it works well as both a celebratory dinner or a simple weeknight dinner in.

SUBSTITUTIONS

Steak: Chicken breasts or thighs, pork chops, or sliced portobello mushrooms for a vegetarian option

Zucchini: Yellow squash, green beans, or small broccoli florets

Campari tomatoes: Grape or cherry tomatoes or 1 (14.5-ounce) can diced tomatoes

Fresh sage: 1 teaspoon dry sage, fresh thyme or rosemary, or omit

EQUIPMENT & LEFTOVERS

You'll need: Paper towel and large oven-safe skillet

Leftovers: Store leftovers in the fridge for 3–4 days

INGREDIENTS

1 pound steak (such as skirt, bavette, flank, rib eye, or hanger)

Salt and pepper to taste

2 tablespoons neutral cooking oil

1 yellow onion, peeled and diced

8 ounces cremini mushrooms, trimmed and thinly sliced

3 zucchini, trimmed and small-diced

6 cloves garlic, peeled and minced

1 pound Campari tomatoes, quartered

A few shakes of paprika, optional

10 sage leaves, half thinly sliced and half left whole

2 tablespoons butter, optional

METHOD

1. **Sear the steak:** Pat the steak dry and season all over with salt and pepper. Preheat oven to 375°F. In a large oven-safe skillet, heat 2 tablespoons cooking oil over high heat. Once the oil is very hot and shimmering, add steak and cook without moving for 2 minutes. Flip and cook an additional 2 minutes. If the steak has a fat cap, flip the steak up on its side and cook the fat for 1 minute more. If either side of the steak doesn't look seared enough, flip it on that side for another 15 to 30 seconds max. Transfer to a plate.

2. **Cook the vegetables:** Heat the skillet to medium and add the onion and mushrooms. Cook, stirring often, for 7 to 8 minutes or until the mushrooms begin to deepen in color. Add zucchini and cook an additional 5 minutes, stirring often. Add minced garlic and cook for 30 seconds. Add the tomatoes and cook for 2 minutes more. Season all over with salt, pepper, and paprika. Add both the sliced and whole sage leaves and toss to combine. Push the vegetables over to one side of the skillet and turn off the heat.

3. **Roast the steak:** Place the steak on the opposite side of the vegetables and transfer to the oven for 2 minutes. Turn off the heat and leave the skillet in the warm oven for 6 to 7 minutes more or until desired internal temperature is reached.

4. **Broil the steak, optional:** Remove skillet from the oven and transfer to the stove. Turn the broiler on. Once it is hot, place the butter on top of the steak and transfer the entire skillet to the broiler for 2 minutes or until the butter melts into the steak to create a crispy, golden-brown crust on top.

5. **To serve:** Slice the steak against the grain and serve on top of the vegetables. Enjoy!

PLAN 2: WEEK 4

This seven-day recipe plan includes dinner recipes for five days, all of which serve four. To conquer the grocery store in one shopping trip, the next page outlines a detailed grocery list, with items separated by store department. You will also find storage, freezing, and thawing tips to help you plan your week. Pay special attention to the key players throughout the week (sweet potatoes and arugula) and be sure to buy the freshest and healthiest of those ingredients that you can find, because you will use them for multiple recipes. Store produce in the crisper to keep fresh. Because you'll be using a store-bought rotisserie chicken for the gnocchi soup, cook that recipe on Monday to ensure you're eating the chicken at its freshest. Since you'll be using sweet potatoes in multiple recipes, be sure to choose large, firm sweet potatoes and store them in a cool, dark, and well-ventilated place.

THE MENU

MONDAY
Easy Creamy Chicken
Gnocchi Soup

TUESDAY
Baked Sweet Potatoes with Black
Bean Chili

WEDNESDAY
Spicy Sesame Sweet Potato Bowl

THURSDAY
Smoked Trout Salad with
Lemon-Honey Vinaigrette

FRIDAY
Steak Tartines with Horseradish Aioli,
Cheese, and Arugula

PLAN 2: WEEK 4
CONQUERING THE GROCERY STORE

FOOD SAFETY GUIDELINES
Buying groceries for the entire week can require some forethought, so be sure to refer to the FDA's storage and freezing guidelines for raw ingredients. All fish, chicken, and steak require twenty-four hours to thaw out in the fridge.

Raw fish, shellfish, chicken, and ground meats: Store in fridge for 1–2 days
Steak and pork (roasts and chops): Store in fridge for 3–5 days
Uncooked, unopened bacon: Store in fridge for 1–2 weeks

PROTEIN
- ☐ 8 ounces smoked trout, skin removed
- ☐ 1 pound flank or skirt steak
- ☐ 1 store-bought rotisserie chicken

GRAIN
- ☐ 2 cups uncooked white rice
- ☐ 16 ounces gnocchi

OIL
- ☐ Extra-virgin olive oil
- ☐ Cooking oil

DAIRY
- ☐ 1 cup heavy cream
- ☐ ¼ cup shaved Parmesan cheese
- ☐ 1 cup shredded cheddar cheese
- ☐ 1 tablespoon butter, optional

STOCK
- ☐ 6 cups low-sodium chicken stock
- ☐ 2 cups low-sodium vegetable stock

FRUITS & VEGETABLES
- ☐ 6 sweet potatoes
- ☐ 2 bell peppers (red, green, or yellow)
- ☐ 3 red bell peppers
- ☐ 4 carrots
- ☐ 2 parsnips
- ☐ 1 lime
- ☐ 5 ounces baby spinach
- ☐ 15 ounces arugula
- ☐ 1 pint cherry tomatoes
- ☐ 3 yellow onions
- ☐ 3 lemons
- ☐ 10 cloves garlic
- ☐ 1 cup fresh parsley
- ☐ 1-inch piece of ginger
- ☐ 1 avocado

PANTRY & SPICES

- ☐ 4 thick slices sourdough bread or sandwich bread of your choice
- ☐ 1 (14.5-ounce) can fire-roasted crushed tomatoes
- ☐ 1 (15-ounce) can black beans
- ☐ 1 can chipotles in adobo sauce
- ☐ ½ cup shelled walnuts
- ☐ Mayonnaise
- ☐ Soy sauce
- ☐ Sambal oolek
- ☐ Sesame oil
- ☐ Prepared horseradish
- ☐ Honey
- ☐ Whole-grain mustard
- ☐ Cumin
- ☐ Dry thyme
- ☐ Chili powder
- ☐ Paprika
- ☐ Garlic powder
- ☐ Onion powder
- ☐ Salt
- ☐ Pepper
- ☐ Crushed red pepper
- ☐ Korean chili threads, optional
- ☐ Sesame seeds

TIP

To speed up the thawing process, place the frozen protein in a resealable storage bag and push out the air before sealing the bag. Place the bag in a bowl and run cold water over the bag. Fill the bowl with water and use a heavy jar (such as peanut butter) to keep the bag submerged below the water. Replace the water every ten minutes with more cold water. Alternatively, allow the water to run at a very slow rate. This will take anywhere from thirty minutes to an hour. Note: To keep bacteria from forming, the water must be at 40°F. If using standing water, do not allow the water to reach room temperature.

Easy Creamy Chicken Gnocchi Soup

Time to Make: 45 minutes

Serves: 4

WHY THIS RECIPE WORKS

This is such a versatile chicken soup recipe. Our shortcut? Use a store-bought rotisserie chicken. If your local grocer doesn't sell rotisserie chickens, simply cube up boneless skinless chicken breasts but adjust the cook time as necessary to ensure they are cooked through.

SUBSTITUTIONS

Rotisserie chicken: Cubed boneless skinless chicken breasts or 1 (15-ounce) can of cannellini beans

Gnocchi: 1 cup shells or farfalle (cook time may vary)

EQUIPMENT & LEFTOVERS

You'll Need: Soup pot

Leftovers: Store leftovers in the fridge for up to 3 days

INGREDIENTS

1 tablespoon cooking oil

1 large yellow onion, peeled and diced

1 red bell pepper, trimmed, deseeded, and diced

4 cloves garlic, peeled and minced

Salt and pepper to taste

1 store-bought rotisserie chicken, meat picked and shredded and bones discarded

6 cups low-sodium chicken stock

4 carrots, peeled and sliced into rounds

2 parsnips, peeled and sliced into rounds

1 teaspoon dry thyme

1 teaspoon paprika

Crushed red pepper to taste

16 ounces fresh gnocchi

½ cup heavy cream

1 lemon, juiced

1 cup fresh parsley, roughly chopped, a pinch or two reserved for garnish

Extra-virgin olive oil, optional, for garnish

(Continued on page 115)

METHOD

1. **Prepare the soup base:** In a soup pot, heat the oil over medium heat until hot. Add onion and red bell pepper and cook, stirring often, until softened and well-browned, about 8 minutes. Add garlic and cook for 1 minute until fragrant. Season with salt and pepper. Add the shredded chicken and toss to combine. Cook until the chicken begins to brown slightly, about 4 minutes. Pour in the chicken stock and scrape up any browned bits stuck to the bottom. Add the carrots and parsnips. Season with salt, pepper, thyme, paprika, and crushed red pepper. Bring to a boil and then reduce heat and simmer for 30 minutes or until the carrots and parsnips are fork tender.

2. **Cook the gnocchi:** Turn the soup back to a low boil and add the gnocchi. Cook for 1 to 3 minutes or until all the gnocchi begin to float and are soft and tender. Turn off the heat.

3. **Finish the soup:** Pour in the heavy cream, lemon juice, and all but a pinch or two of fresh parsley leaves. Cook for 1 to 2 more minutes to allow the flavors to meld. Do not overcook.

4. **To serve:** Ladle chicken gnocchi soup into bowls and garnish each bowl with the reserved chopped parsley leaves. Drizzle with extra-virgin olive oil, if desired. Enjoy!

Baked Sweet Potatoes with Black Bean Chili

Time to Make: 45–50 minutes

Serves: 4

WHY THIS RECIPE WORKS

Baked sweet potatoes take a bit of time to cook in the oven, which gives you plenty of time to prepare a spicy vegetarian black bean chili. If you're concerned about heat, replace chipotles in adobo sauce with a small can of adobo sauce. It will be less spicy but will still add a touch of heat and flavor to the chili and the crema.

SUBSTITUTIONS

Sweet potatoes: Russet potatoes

Chipotles in adobo sauce: Adobo sauce or omit and use a sprinkle of cayenne powder in the crema

Black beans: Kidney or pinto beans

Sour cream: Greek yogurt

EQUIPMENT & LEFTOVERS

You'll Need: Aluminum foil, baking sheet, medium pot

Leftovers: Store leftover crema, sweet potatoes, and chili in separate containers in the fridge for up to 5 days.

INGREDIENTS

4 sweet potatoes

1 can chipotles in adobo sauce

2 teaspoons cooking oil

1 yellow onion, peeled and diced

2 bell peppers, trimmed, deseeded, and small-diced

1 tablespoon cumin

1 tablespoon chili powder

2 teaspoons paprika

1 teaspoon garlic powder

½ teaspoon onion powder

1 (15-ounce) can black beans, drained and rinsed

1 (14.5-ounce) can fire-roasted crushed tomatoes

½ cup water

4 ounces sour cream

1 lime, quartered

5 ounces baby spinach

Sprinkle of salt

Dry chives, optional, for garnish

(Continued on next page)

METHOD

1. **Prepare sweet potatoes:** Preheat oven to 425°F. Scrub potatoes, then prick all over with a fork. Transfer to a foil-lined baking sheet, then place in the oven for 45 to 50 minutes or until sweet potatoes are tender and cooked through. Allow the sweet potatoes to cool for a few minutes.

2. **Prepare chipotles in adobo sauce:** Remove 1 to 2 of the chipotle peppers (or more, if you prefer a spicier chili) from the can of chipotles in adobo sauce and finely chop them.

3. **Prepare the black bean chili:** Heat 2 teaspoons oil in a medium pot. Add the diced onion and diced bell peppers and cook until softened, about 5 to 7 minutes. Add the cumin, chili powder, paprika, garlic powder, and onion powder, and stir until the vegetables are coated in the spices. Add the drained black beans along with a can of tomatoes, chopped chipotle peppers, and ½ cup water. Bring to a boil and then simmer until the sweet potatoes have finished baking.

4. **Prepare the chipotle crema:** Combine the sour cream with 1 to 2 teaspoons of the adobo sauce from the can of chipotles in adobo. If you prefer a spicier crema, add more adobo sauce to taste. Discard or reserve the remaining chipotles in adobo sauce for another use. Thin out the crema with a tablespoon or two of water and season with salt, to taste.

5. **To serve:** Cut the sweet potatoes open and divide the baby spinach between four plates. Squeeze lime juice over the spinach on each plate and add a sprinkle of salt. Place a baked sweet potato on each plate and spoon the chili on top. Serve with chipotle crema and a sprinkle of dry chives. Enjoy!

Spicy Sesame Sweet Potato Bowl

Time to Make: 30–40 minutes

Serves: 4

WHY THIS RECIPE WORKS

The base of this sweet potato bowl is simple: onions, garlic, and ginger for aromatics combined with sesame, soy, honey, and sambal oolek for a sweet, spicy, salty flavor that pairs perfectly with fluffy white rice. The final product is a brothy sweet potato bowl that you can whip up any day of the week. If you're watching carbs, serve these spicy sesame sweet potatoes with roasted peppers and broccoli or simply sauté any choice of vegetables with the sweet potatoes.

SUBSTITUTIONS

White rice: Brown or wild rice, cooking time will vary

Sweet potatoes: Use your favorite vegetables, such as broccoli, green beans, baby corn, or bell peppers

EQUIPMENT & LEFTOVERS

You'll need: Saucepan with lid, wide skillet

Leftovers: Store leftovers in the fridge for up to 3–5 days

INGREDIENTS

2 cups uncooked white rice

4 cups water

1 tablespoon butter, optional

Salt and pepper to taste

2 teaspoons cooking oil

1 yellow onion, peeled and diced

6 cloves garlic, peeled and minced

1-inch piece of ginger, peeled and minced

2 sweet potatoes, peeled and small-diced

2 tablespoons soy sauce

2 tablespoons chili garlic sauce

2 tablespoons honey

1 tablespoon sesame oil plus extra for garnish

2 cups low-sodium vegetable stock

1 avocado

Chili threads or crushed red pepper, optional, for garnish

Sesame seeds, for garnish

(Continued on page 121)

METHOD

1. **Prepare the rice:** In a saucepan, combine the rice, 4 cups water, butter (if using), and salt. Bring to a boil and stir once. Reduce heat, cover, and simmer for 15 to 20 minutes. Turn off the heat and let the rice rest for 5 to 10 minutes before removing the lid.

2. **Start the aromatics:** Add 2 teaspoons of cooking oil to a skillet over medium heat. Once hot, add diced onion and cook, stirring regularly, for 5 minutes until softened and beginning to brown. Add the garlic and ginger and cook for 45 seconds until fragrant.

3. **Cook the sweet potato:** Add the diced sweet potatoes to the skillet and cook, stirring regularly, for 8 to 10 minutes until the sweet potatoes begin to soften and caramelize around the edges.

4. **Prepare the sauce:** To the same skillet, add soy sauce, chili garlic sauce, honey, and sesame oil, and stir to coat the sweet potatoes. Add vegetable stock and scrape up any browned bits stuck to the bottom of the skillet.

5. **Finish the sweet potatoes:** Bring to a boil, reduce heat, and simmer for 10 minutes until the sweet potato is softened. Add more stock or water as desired. Season to taste with salt and pepper.

6. **To serve:** Right before serving, peel the avocado and remove the pit. Thinly slice the avocado. Divide the cooked rice between bowls and spoon the broth and sweet potatoes on top. Arrange avocado and chili threads (or crushed red pepper) on top and finish with a sprinkle of sesame seeds and a drizzle of sesame oil, if desired. Enjoy!

Smoked Trout Salad with Lemon-Honey Vinaigrette

Time to Make: 20 minutes

Serves: 4

WHY THIS RECIPE WORKS

This is a perfect midweek respite that adds fresh greens and tomatoes to your plate with a sweet and tangy lemon-honey vinaigrette. Paired with flaked smoked trout, this recipe is a combination of sweet, salty, and bright.

SUBSTITUTIONS

Smoked trout: Any smoked seafood such as salmon, mussels, or scallops

Arugula: Baby spinach or torn lettuce

EQUIPMENT & LEFTOVERS

You'll need: A large mixing bowl, zester, whisk

Leftovers: The salad should be enjoyed immediately

INGREDIENTS

1 lemon, juice and zest

2 tablespoons honey

2 teaspoons whole-grain mustard

⅓ cup plus 2 teaspoons extra-virgin olive oil

Salt and pepper to taste

10 ounces arugula

1 pint cherry tomatoes, halved

½ cup shelled walnuts, roughly chopped

8 ounces skinless smoked trout, flaked into bite-size pieces

¼ cup shaved Parmesan cheese

METHOD

1. **Prepare the lemon-honey vinaigrette:** Add the lemon juice and zest to a bowl. Add the honey and whole-grain mustard and stir to combine. Slowly whisk in the extra-virgin olive oil until emulsified. Taste and season with salt and pepper.

2. **Prepare the salad:** In a large bowl, combine the arugula, halved cherry tomatoes, and walnuts and drizzle with 2 teaspoons extra-virgin olive oil and a sprinkle of salt and pepper.

3. **To serve:** Divide the dressed salad between bowls and arrange the trout and shaved Parmesan cheese on top. Drizzle each salad with lemon-honey vinaigrette. Enjoy!

Steak Tartines with Horseradish Aioli, Cheese, and Arugula

Time to Make: About 40 minutes

Serves: 4

WHY THIS RECIPE WORKS

Serving these tartines with simply dressed greens will counterbalance the richness of the aioli, cheese, and steak, making this a dinner that is rich without being overly decadent.

SUBSTITUTIONS

Steak: Boneless, skinless chicken breasts cut into cubes

Arugula: Baby spinach

Mayonnaise: Greek yogurt or sour cream

EQUIPMENT & LEFTOVERS

You'll need: Paper towel, sheet pan, skillet

Leftovers: Only assemble the number of tartines needed for dinner. Store leftover ingredients separately for up to 3–4 days.

INGREDIENTS

5 ounces arugula

3 teaspoons extra-virgin olive oil plus more as needed

1 small lemon, juice

Salt and pepper to taste

2 teaspoons prepared horseradish or more or less to taste

2 tablespoons mayonnaise

4 thick slices sourdough bread or sandwich bread of your choice

2 red bell peppers, trimmed, deseeded, and thinly sliced

1 tablespoon cooking oil

1 pound steak such as flank, skirt, or boneless rib eye

1 cup shredded cheddar cheese

METHOD

1. **Dress the arugula:** In a bowl, toss the arugula with 1 teaspoon extra-virgin olive oil and lemon juice and season lightly with salt and pepper. Keep in the fridge until ready to serve.

2. **Prepare horseradish aioli:** In a small bowl, combine the horseradish, mayonnaise, and 1 teaspoon of extra-virgin olive oil. Season with salt and pepper if desired. Mix until smooth and creamy and set aside. Add more horseradish if you want a punchier mayonnaise.

3. **Prepare the bread and bell peppers:** Brush the bread lightly with extra-virgin olive oil on both sides and season with salt and pepper. Arrange on one side of a baking sheet. Place the sliced peppers on the other side of the baking sheet and drizzle with 1 teaspoon extra-virgin olive oil and season with salt and pepper. (Note: Use 2 baking sheets if one isn't large enough.) Transfer to the oven and bake for 10 minutes. Flip and roast an additional 10 minutes or until bread is golden brown all over and the peppers have softened. Remove the pan from the oven and turn the broiler on. Leave the toasted bread and the peppers on the sheet pan, as you will reuse the pan.

4. **Prepare the steak:** Add 1 tablespoon cooking oil to a skillet and turn the heat to high. Once the oil is very hot and shimmering, add steak but do not

(Continued on next page)

overcrowd the pan; cook in batches if necessary. Cook steak without moving for 2 minutes and then flip and cook an additional 2 minutes or until the steak is just cooked through and the pieces have begun to form a crust. Transfer to a bowl and set aside.

5. **Assemble the steak tartines:** Spread 1 teaspoon of the horseradish aioli evenly on each slice of bread. Divide the shredded cheese between each slice of bread. Next, add the roasted bell peppers on top of the cheese. Finally, pile the steak on top of each piece of toast. Transfer to the broiler for 2 to 3 minutes or until cheese is melted and the steak is golden brown on top. Remove from the broiler.

6. **To serve:** Sprinkle a few pieces of dressed arugula on top of each steak tartine. Arrange the remaining arugula on 4 plates and serve a tartine next to each salad. Serve with more horseradish aioli on top, if desired. Enjoy!

PLAN 3: WEEK 1

This seven-day recipe plan includes dinner recipes for five days, all of which serve four. To conquer the grocery store in one shopping trip, the next page outlines a detailed grocery list, with items separated by store department. You will also find storage, freezing, and thawing tips to help you plan your week. This plan is all about reusing! If you have excess fennel fronds as you prepare the tortellini soup, save them for the fennel and tomato salad, or you can even sprinkle them on the shaved carrot and beet salad. You will also whip up more dressing than you need for the Charred Fennel and Tomato Salad, but be sure to save the leftovers, so you can reuse the dressing for the shaved carrot and beet salad. Pay special attention to the key players throughout the week (fresh fennel, golden beets, and ricotta cheese) and be sure to buy the freshest and healthiest of those ingredients that you can find, because you will use them for multiple recipes. Store the fresh vegetables in the crisper.

THE MENU

MONDAY
Tortellini Soup with Fennel

TUESDAY
Ricotta and Pork Meatball Soup

WEDNESDAY
Charred Fennel and Tomato Salad

THURSDAY
Golden Beet Ragù with Polenta

FRIDAY
Shaved Carrot and Beet Salad with
Herbed Ricotta

PLAN 3: WEEK 1
CONQUERING THE GROCERY STORE

FOOD SAFETY GUIDELINES

Buying groceries for the entire week can require some forethought, so be sure to refer to the FDA's storage and freezing guidelines for raw ingredients. All fish, chicken, and steak require twenty-four hours to thaw out in the fridge.

Raw fish, shellfish, chicken, and ground meats: Store in fridge for 1–2 days
Steak and pork (roasts and chops): Store in fridge for 3–5 days
Uncooked, unopened bacon: Store in fridge for 1–2 weeks

PROTEIN
- ☐ 1 pound ground pork
- ☐ 12 ounces bacon

GRAIN
- ☐ 12 ounces store-bought fresh tortellini
- ☐ ½ cup polenta or coarsely ground yellow cornmeal

OIL
- ☐ Cooking oil
- ☐ Extra-virgin olive oil

DAIRY
- ☐ 2 cups ricotta cheese
- ☐ ½ cup freshly grated Parmesan cheese, plus more, if desired

STOCK
- ☐ 6 cups low-sodium chicken stock
- ☐ 7 cups low-sodium vegetable stock

FRUITS & VEGETABLES
- ☐ 3 yellow onions
- ☐ 14 carrots
- ☐ 3 fennel bulbs, with stems and fronds
- ☐ ½ pound fingerling potatoes
- ☐ ½ pound baby gold potatoes (or fingerling)
- ☐ 1 bunch lacinato kale
- ☐ 1 bunch escarole
- ☐ 1 bunch green leaf lettuce
- ☐ 10 ounces baby greens
- ☐ 1 pint cherry tomatoes
- ☐ 8 Campari tomatoes
- ☐ ¾ cup fresh parsley leaves
- ☐ 1 lemon
- ☐ 4 golden beets
- ☐ 8 ounces cremini mushrooms
- ☐ 6 cloves garlic

(Continued on next page)

PANTRY & SPICES

- ☐ 1 (14.5-ounce) can diced tomatoes
- ☐ 1 (14.5-ounce) can crushed tomatoes
- ☐ Bread crumbs
- ☐ Whole-grain Dijon mustard
- ☐ Honey
- ☐ Tomato paste
- ☐ Ground nutmeg
- ☐ Dry rosemary
- ☐ Dry thyme
- ☐ Dry chives
- ☐ Dry parsley
- ☐ Dry basil
- ☐ Golden raisins
- ☐ Pumpkin seeds
- ☐ Salt and pepper
- ☐ Crushed red pepper

TIP

To speed up the thawing process, place the frozen protein in a resealable storage bag and push out the air before sealing the bag. Place the bag in a bowl and run cold water over the bag. Fill the bowl with water and use a heavy jar (such as peanut butter) to keep the bag submerged below the water. Replace the water every ten minutes with more cold water. Alternatively, allow the water to run at a very slow rate. This will take anywhere from thirty minutes to an hour. Note: To keep bacteria from forming, the water must be at 40°F. If using standing water, do not allow the water to reach room temperature.

Tortellini Soup with Fennel

Time to Make: 45 minutes

Serves: 4

WHY THIS RECIPE WORKS

This simple, fragrant weeknight soup recipe uses all the flavors of fennel, from the bulb to the stems and fronds, to build an aromatic and tasty soup with no wasted fennel. If you have excess fennel fronds, save them for the Charred Fennel and Tomato Salad (page 135) later in the week!

SUBSTITUTIONS

Fennel: If your store doesn't carry fresh fennel, simply omit and add more potatoes or a can of drained red kidney beans or cannellini beans

Escarole: Baby spinach, lacinato kale, or arugula

EQUIPMENT & LEFTOVERS

You'll need: Soup pot, skillet

Leftovers: Store leftovers in the fridge for 3–4 days

INGREDIENTS

1 large fennel bulb, with stems and fronds

2 tablespoons cooking oil, divided

1 yellow onion, peeled and diced

3 carrots, peeled and diced

½ pound fingerling potatoes, halved

Salt and pepper to taste

6 cups low-sodium vegetable stock

1 (14.5-ounce) can diced tomatoes

Crushed red pepper, to taste

12 ounces store-bought fresh tortellini

1 bunch escarole, torn into bite-size pieces

Extra-virgin olive oil, optional, for garnish

METHOD

1. **Prepare the fennel:** Pick the fennel fronds from the stems and set aside for garnish. Cut the fennel stems from the bulb and thinly slice the stems into rounds. Cut the bulb in half and cut out the core and discard.

2. **Fry the aromatics:** Heat 1 tablespoon oil in a soup pot over medium-high until very hot. Add diced onion and cook, stirring often, for 3 to 4 minutes or until beginning to soften. Add carrots, sliced fennel stems, and the potatoes and cook for 5 to 6 minutes or until beginning to brown all over. Season with salt and pepper. Pour in the vegetable stock and the diced tomatoes and bring to a boil. Reduce heat and simmer for 20 to 25 minutes or until potatoes are fork tender. Taste and season with salt, pepper, and crushed red pepper to taste.

3. **Cook the fennel:** Meanwhile, heat the remaining 1 tablespoon oil in a skillet over medium-high. Once the skillet is very hot, add the sliced fennel bulb and cook in an even layer without moving for 2 to 3 minutes or until beginning to char. Flip and cook an additional 2 to 3 minutes or until golden brown all over and beginning to char around the edges. Turn off the heat and sprinkle the fennel with a bit of salt. Set aside and keep warm.

4. **Finish the soup:** Bring the soup back to a boil and add the tortellini and escarole. Cook until the escarole is wilted and the tortellini is al dente, about 5 minutes.

5. **To serve:** Ladle the soup into bowls and arrange the fried fennel on top. Garnish with the reserved fennel fronds and drizzle with a touch of extra-virgin olive oil, if desired. Enjoy!

Ricotta and Pork Meatball Soup

Time to Make: 45 minutes (20 minutes inactive)

Serves: 4

WHY THIS RECIPE WORKS

Thanks to ricotta cheese, the meatballs in this soup are moist and decadent with the perfect amount of sweet spice from a few shakes of nutmeg.

SUBSTITUTIONS

Ground pork: Ground chicken, ground turkey, or ground beef

Lacinato kale: Baby spinach, escarole, or arugula

Bread crumbs: Panko or crushed crackers (such as saltines or butter crackers)

EQUIPMENT & LEFTOVERS

You'll need: Large bowl, wide soup pot

Leftovers: Store leftovers in the fridge for 3–4 days

INGREDIENTS

1 pound ground pork

½ cup ricotta cheese

¼ cup freshly grated Parmesan cheese, plus more for garnish, if desired

¼ cup bread crumbs, plus more if needed

½ cup fresh parsley leaves, roughly chopped, divided

½ teaspoon ground nutmeg

Salt, pepper, crushed red pepper to taste

1 tablespoon cooking oil

1 yellow onion, peeled and diced

4 carrots, peeled and cut into rounds on an angle

½ pound baby gold potatoes (or fingerling), halved

1 pint cherry tomatoes

6 cups low-sodium chicken stock, plus more if desired

1 teaspoon dry rosemary

1 teaspoon dry thyme

1 bunch lacinato kale, thick center rib removed and leaves roughly chopped

Extra-virgin olive oil, optional, for garnish

(Continued on next page)

METHOD

1. **Prepare the meatballs:** In a large bowl, combine the ground pork, ricotta cheese, grated Parmesan cheese, bread crumbs, half of the chopped parsley leaves, and the ground nutmeg. Season with salt, pepper and a shake of crushed red pepper if desired. Combine the mixture with your hands, being careful not to overmix the meatballs. Form the mixture into 2-inch meatballs; do not over-roll the meatballs. Transfer them to a plate and store in the fridge.

2. **Sauté the vegetables:** Heat 1 tablespoon cooking oil in a wide soup pot over medium-high. Add the onion and cook, stirring often, for 5 minutes until softened and beginning to brown. Add carrots, potatoes, and tomatoes and cook for an additional 5 minutes. Season all over with salt and pepper.

3. **Prepare the soup:** Pour in the chicken stock and bring to a boil. Season with salt, pepper, crushed red pepper, dry rosemary (crush the rosemary between your fingers as you add it), and dry thyme. Carefully drop the meatballs into the soup pot. Reduce heat to medium and cook, uncovered, over a very low boil for 20 minutes or until potatoes are fork-tender and the meatballs are cooked through. Add more stock if a brothy soup is your preference. Taste and season.

4. **Finish the soup:** Add the kale and the remaining fresh parsley, gently folding it into the broth. Cover and cook for 5 minutes longer or until the kale is wilted. Turn off the heat.

5. **To serve:** Ladle ricotta meatballs and the soup between bowls. Drizzle with a touch of extra-virgin olive oil, if desired, and sprinkle each bowl with Parmesan cheese. Enjoy!

Charred Fennel and Tomato Salad

Time to Make: 35 minutes

Serves: 4

WHY THIS RECIPE WORKS

Charring the tomatoes and fennel enhances their flavors in this easy, bold salad option. This salad is so delicious on its own but also works well served over crisp greens, such as green leaf lettuce or chopped romaine. If you have any excess reserved fronds from the Tortellini Soup with Fennel (page 131), use them as a garnish on this salad! Be sure to save the extra dressing for the Golden Beet Ragù with Polenta (page 139) later on in the week.

SUBSTITUTIONS

Fennel: If your store doesn't carry fresh fennel, simply swap it with another vegetable that is amenable to charring, such as diced sweet potatoes, carrots, or zucchini

Green leaf lettuce: Baby spinach, lacinato kale, or arugula

Campari tomatoes: Small tomatoes on the vine

EQUIPMENT & LEFTOVERS

You'll need: Medium bowl, whisk, skillet

Leftovers: Store leftovers in the fridge for 3–4 days

INGREDIENTS

2 fennel bulbs, with stems and fronds

1 lemon, juiced

1 tablespoon whole-grain Dijon mustard

1 tablespoon honey

¾ cup extra-virgin olive oil

Salt and pepper to taste

12 ounces bacon, sliced into lardons

8 Campari tomatoes, quartered

1 bunch green leaf lettuce, roughly chopped

(Continued on page 137)

METHOD

1. **Prepare the fennel:** Remove the fronds from the fennel stems and set aside. Slice the bulbs in half and remove the core. Thinly slice the bulbs.

2. **Prepare the vinaigrette:** To a medium bowl, add lemon juice, mustard, and honey and whisk until incorporated. While whisking, slowly pour in the extra-virgin olive oil and continue whisking until emulsified. Season with salt and pepper and set aside.

3. **Fry the bacon:** Sprinkle the bacon in an even layer in a large skillet. Turn the heat to medium and cook, stirring often, until the bacon is crispy and well-browned all over, about 8 to 10 minutes. Using a slotted spoon, scoop the bacon out of the skillet and transfer to a bowl. Turn the heat on the bacon fat to medium-high.

4. **Char the fennel:** To the hot bacon fat, add the sliced fennel in an even layer (cook in batches, if necessary). Cook without moving for 2 minutes or until golden brown and beginning to char. Flip and cook an additional 2 minutes or until charred on the other side. Transfer the fennel to a large bowl and sprinkle with salt.

5. **Char the tomatoes:** In the same skillet, add the tomatoes cut-side down and cook without moving for 2 to 3 minutes or until beginning to char. Flip and cook an additional 2 to 3 minutes until charred on the other side. Transfer to the bowl of fennel and season with salt.

6. **To serve:** Arrange the chopped lettuce on plates and pile the fennel and tomatoes on top. Sprinkle the bacon and reserved fennel fronds on top of each plate and drizzle each salad with vinaigrette. Enjoy!

Golden Beet Ragù with Polenta

Time to Make: 45 minutes

Serves: 4

WHY THIS RECIPE WORKS

Rich polenta pairs perfectly with this healthy, vegetable-packed ragù. The natural sugars in golden beets tone down the acidity of the canned tomatoes.

SUBSTITUTIONS

Golden beets: Red beets, sweet potatoes, or butternut squash

Ricotta cheese: Sour cream or heavy cream

EQUIPMENT & LEFTOVERS

You'll need: Wide pot, saucepan, whisk

Leftovers: Store leftovers in the fridge for 3–4 days

INGREDIENTS

1 tablespoon cooking oil

1 yellow onion, peeled and diced

3 carrots, peeled and small-diced

2 medium golden beets, trimmed, peeled, and small-diced

Salt, pepper, and crushed red pepper to taste

8 ounces cremini mushrooms, scrubbed and quartered

6 cloves garlic, peeled and minced

¼ cup fresh parsley, finely chopped

2 tablespoons tomato paste

1 cup low-sodium vegetable stock

1 (14.5-ounce) can crushed tomatoes

1 teaspoon dry thyme

3 cups water

1 cup polenta or coarsely ground yellow cornmeal

1 cup ricotta cheese

¼ cup fresh grated Parmesan cheese, plus more for garnish if desired

Fresh parsley leaves, for garnish

(Continued on next page)

METHOD

1. **Start the ragù:** In a wide pot, heat the oil over medium-high until very hot. Add the onion, carrots, and golden beets. Cook, stirring often, until beginning to brown around the edges and soften, about 5 minutes. Adjust the heat as necessary to keep the vegetables from burning. Season with salt, pepper, and crushed red pepper to taste. Add mushrooms and cook until they begin to brown, about 5 minutes more. Add garlic and cook for 45 seconds until fragrant. Add the tomato paste and coat the vegetables in the paste. Cook for 1 to 2 minutes until the paste begins to deepen in color. Stir in the vegetable stock and scrape up any browned bits stuck to the bottom. Continue stirring until the sauce is smooth and velvety. Add the crushed tomatoes along with salt, pepper, and thyme. Bring to a boil and then reduce heat and simmer for 20 minutes to allow the flavors to meld. Taste and season to your preferences.

2. **Prepare the polenta:** While the ragù is simmering, in a saucepan bring 3 cups of water to a boil over medium-high heat. Once the water is boiling, sprinkle the polenta over the water, whisking to incorporate it. Add a sprinkle of salt and cook for 10 minutes, whisking frequently to break up any lumps. Adjust the heat as necessary if the polenta is becoming unwieldy! Once the polenta is tender, whisk in the ricotta cheese and Parmesan cheese. Taste and season to your preferences with salt and pepper. Turn off the heat.

3. **To serve:** Divide the cooked polenta between bowls and ladle the golden beet ragù on top. Garnish with more Parmesan cheese and a sprinkle of fresh parsley leaves, if desired. Enjoy!

Shaved Carrot and Beet Salad with Herbed Ricotta

Time to Make: 20 minutes

Serves: 4

WHY THIS RECIPE WORKS

Use up the remaining ricotta cheese in this simple, bright salad with quickly marinated golden beets and carrots. This recipe will also use the remaining Dijon vinaigrette from the Charred Fennel and Tomato Salad (page 135) earlier in the week!

SUBSTITUTIONS

Golden beets: Red beets, sweet potatoes, or butternut squash

Pumpkin seeds: Sunflower seeds or any nut variety you prefer

EQUIPMENT & LEFTOVERS

You'll need: Vegetable peeler, large mixing bowl

Leftovers: This salad should be enjoyed immediately.

INGREDIENTS

1 cup ricotta cheese

1 tablespoon plus 1 teaspoon extra-virgin olive oil

1 teaspoon dry chives

1 teaspoon dry parsley

½ teaspoon dry basil

Salt and pepper to taste

4 carrots, trimmed and peeled

2 golden beets, trimmed and peeled

½ cup golden raisins

10 ounces baby greens

1 cup pumpkin seeds

(Continued on page 143)

METHOD

1. **Prepare the herbed ricotta:** Combine ricotta cheese with 1 teaspoon extra-virgin olive oil and the dry chives, parsley, and basil. Taste and season with salt and pepper. Set aside.

2. **Prepare the carrots and golden beets:** Using a vegetable peeler, shave the carrots into ribbons. Cut the golden beets in half lengthwise and then use a sharp knife to slice each half into paper-thin half-moons.

3. **Prepare the salad:** In a large mixing bowl, add the golden raisins and the baby greens. Drizzle with 1 tablespoon extra-virgin olive oil and sprinkle with salt and pepper. Toss to coat. Carefully roll the carrot ribbons into loose rosettes around your finger or the handle of a wooden spoon and set aside.

4. **To serve:** Divide the dressed salad greens between bowls. Arrange the carrot rosettes on top and fan out a few golden beet slices around the salad. Place a dollop of herbed ricotta cheese and ¼ cup pumpkin seeds in the middle of each salad. Drizzle with the Dijon vinaigrette and a sprinkle of salt and pepper. Enjoy!

PLAN 3: WEEK 2

This seven-day recipe plan includes dinner recipes for five days, all of which serve four. To conquer the grocery store in one shopping trip, the next page outlines a detailed grocery list, with items separated by store department. You will also find storage, freezing, and thawing tips to help you plan your week. This plan loads up on the spice, but if you're not amenable to spicy meals, you have plenty of opportunity to temper the heat as necessary by omitting or reducing the amount of spice. Cook the Black Lentils with Asparagus with Poached Eggs first, since asparagus has a shorter refrigerator life than other vegetables. Pay special attention to the key players (acorn squash, fresh cilantro, and fresh jalapeños) throughout the week and be sure to buy the freshest and healthiest of those ingredients that you can find, because you will use them for multiple recipes. Store produce in a bag in the crisper to keep fresh.

THE MENU

MONDAY
Black Lentils and Asparagus
with Poached Eggs

TUESDAY
Chicken Udon Soup with Acorn
Squash and Napa Cabbage

WEDNESDAY
Easy Cilantro-Lime Shrimp Salad

THURSDAY
Spice-Rubbed Acorn Squash
with Spicy Rice

FRIDAY
Pork Chops with Creamy Peas and
Tomatoes

PLAN 3: WEEK 2
CONQUERING THE GROCERY STORE

FOOD SAFETY GUIDELINES

Buying groceries for the entire week can require some forethought, so be sure to refer to the FDA's storage and freezing guidelines for raw ingredients. All fish, chicken, and steak require twenty-four hours to thaw out in the fridge.

Raw fish, shellfish, chicken, and ground meats: Store in fridge for 1–2 days
Steak and pork (roasts and chops): Store in fridge for 3–5 days
Uncooked, unopened bacon: Store in fridge for 1–2 weeks

PROTEIN

- ☐ 6 bone-in, skin-on chicken thighs
- ☐ 1½ pounds large shrimp
- ☐ 4 boneless pork chops, about 1½ inches thick
- ☐ 8 eggs

GRAIN

- ☐ 16 ounces fresh or dry udon noodles
- ☐ 1 cup uncooked brown, wild, or white rice (cook time may vary)

OIL

- ☐ Cooking oil
- ☐ Extra-virgin olive oil

DAIRY

- ☐ 5 tablespoons butter
- ☐ ½ cup heavy cream
- ☐ Grated Gruyère cheese, optional

STOCK

- ☐ 2 cups low-sodium chicken stock

FRUITS & VEGETABLES

- ☐ 1 large Vidalia onion
- ☐ 2 yellow onions
- ☐ 8 cloves garlic
- ☐ 2 acorn squash
- ☐ 1 pound asparagus
- ☐ 2 lemons
- ☐ 2 limes
- ☐ ¼ cup fresh parsley
- ☐ 1½ cup fresh cilantro
- ☐ 7 scallions
- ☐ 1 pint cherry tomatoes
- ☐ 12 ounces fresh or frozen green peas
- ☐ 1 small head napa cabbage
- ☐ 16 ounces baby greens
- ☐ 5–6 jalapeños, depending on heat preference
- ☐ 1 red bell pepper
- ☐ 3 Roma tomatoes
- ☐ 1 English cucumber
- ☐ 1 watermelon radish (or 5 red radishes)

(Continued on next page)

PANTRY & SPICES

- ☐ 1 cup uncooked black lentils
- ☐ 1 (15-ounce) can black beans, drained and rinsed
- ☐ 1 (14.5-ounce) can fire-roasted diced tomatoes
- ☐ Soy sauce
- ☐ Sesame oil
- ☐ Mirin
- ☐ Distilled white vinegar
- ☐ Honey
- ☐ Chili powder
- ☐ Ground cumin
- ☐ Ground black pepper
- ☐ Onion powder
- ☐ Dried oregano
- ☐ Garlic powder
- ☐ Paprika
- ☐ Dry thyme
- ☐ Crushed red pepper, optional
- ☐ Salt
- ☐ Pepper
- ☐ Chili oil, optional
- ☐ Sesame seeds, optional

TIP

To speed up the thawing process, place the frozen protein in a resealable storage bag and push out the air before sealing the bag. Place the bag in a bowl and run cold water over the bag. Fill the bowl with water and use a heavy jar (such as peanut butter) to keep the bag submerged below the water. Replace the water every ten minutes with more cold water. Alternatively, allow the water to run at a very slow rate. This will take anywhere from thirty minutes to an hour. Note: To keep bacteria from forming, the water must be at 40°F. If using standing water, do not allow the water to reach room temperature.

Black Lentils and Asparagus with Poached Eggs

Time to Make: 40 minutes

Serves: 4

WHY THIS RECIPE WORKS

This black lentil salad with poached eggs is supremely versatile, which makes it a great dinner option. Beyond that, black lentils are packed with protein, but the dish doesn't feel heavy, thanks to bright asparagus and sweet, caramelized onions. You will need to poach eight eggs for this recipe. I recommend poaching only four at a time and covering them loosely with foil to keep them warm.

SUBSTITUTIONS

Black lentils: Replace with green lentils, cooking time may vary

Asparagus: Diced sweet potatoes, broccolini, French green beans, or cauliflower florets

Gruyère cheese: Parmesan cheese

EQUIPMENT & LEFTOVERS

You'll need: Medium pot, wide skillet, large bowl, small fine-mesh sieve

Leftovers: Store leftovers in the fridge for 3–4 days

INGREDIENTS

1 cup uncooked black lentils

2½ cups water

1 tablespoon distilled white vinegar

3 tablespoons butter, divided

1 large Vidalia onion, peeled and thinly sliced into rounds

Salt and pepper to taste

1 pound asparagus, woody ends trimmed

8 eggs

¼ cup fresh parsley leaves, finely chopped

1 lemon, juice and zest (keep separate)

1 tablespoon extra-virgin olive oil

Salt and pepper to taste

Grated Gruyère cheese, optional

(Continued on page 149)

METHOD

1. **Prepare black lentils:** Clean and sort dry lentils before cooking. Combine the black lentils and 2½ cups water in a medium pot. Bring to a boil and then reduce heat and simmer for 14 minutes or until the lentils are al dente. Drain and rinse the lentils. (Note: Do not season the lentils with salt until the end of the recipe.) Wipe out the pot and fill it back up with water and return it to the stove with 1 tablespoon distilled white vinegar over low heat.

2. **Prepare the caramelized onions:** While the lentils are cooking, heat 2 tablespoons butter in a wide skillet over medium heat. Once melted and frothy, add the onions and cook, stirring often, for about 15 minutes or until the onions are well-browned all over. Adjust the heat as necessary to ensure even browning without burning the onions. Season with salt and pepper and transfer to a large bowl.

3. **Prepare the asparagus:** Drain off any excess fat from the skillet and return the skillet to the stove. Melt the remaining 1 tablespoon butter over medium heat and add the asparagus spears. Season with salt and pepper and cook, flipping occasionally, for about 5 minutes or until the asparagus spears are just tender and not overcooked. Transfer to a plate and keep warm.

4. **Prepare the poached eggs:** While the asparagus is cooking, crack an egg into a small sieve and strain off as much excess white as possible. Using the back of a spoon, create a whirlpool in a pot of simmering water. Gently ease the egg into the water from the sieve. Continue on with 3 more eggs until 4 eggs are in the pot. While the eggs are poaching, microwave a plate for 1 minute. Check the eggs after 3 to 4 minutes. You should be able to lift them out of the water with a spoon. The whites should be set but not completely solid. Transfer the eggs to the warm plate and cover loosely with foil. Repeat the process with the remaining 4 eggs.

5. **Finish the black lentils:** To the bowl of caramelized onions, add the black lentils, half the chopped parsley leaves, lemon juice, and extra-virgin olive oil and toss to combine. Season with salt and pepper.

6. **To serve:** Divide the cooked asparagus between plates and pile the black lentils on top. Arrange two eggs on each dish and sprinkle with lemon zest and the remaining chopped parsley. Serve with grated Gruyère cheese, if desired.

Chicken Udon Soup with Acorn Squash and Napa Cabbage

Time to Make: 45 minutes

Serves: 4

WHY THIS RECIPE WORKS

Who says you can't have homemade chicken broth on a busy weekday? Thinly sliced acorn squash and napa cabbage work well in a rich and flavorful homemade chicken stock for a soup that is both quick to prepare and booming with flavor.

SUBSTITUTIONS

Acorn squash: Diced butternut squash or sweet potato

Napa cabbage: Green cabbage, red cabbage, baby spinach, or baby bok choy

Chicken thighs: Sliced shiitake mushroom caps or soft tofu

EQUIPMENT & LEFTOVERS

You'll need: Soup pot, large pot

Leftovers: Store leftovers in the fridge for up to 3 days

INGREDIENTS

6 bone-in, skin-on chicken thighs

8 cups water

3 tablespoons soy sauce

1 tablespoon sesame oil

1 tablespoon mirin

16 ounces fresh or dry udon noodles

4 scallions, trimmed and minced, white and green parts separated

1 acorn squash, halved lengthwise and seeds removed, each half thinly sliced

1 small head napa cabbage, trimmed and cut into wide strips

Sesame seeds, optional, for garnish

Chili oil, optional, for garnish

1 jalapeño, sliced, optional, for garnish

METHOD

1. **Prepare the broth:** Cover the chicken thighs with the 8 cups water, soy sauce, sesame oil, and mirin in a soup pot and bring to a boil. Cover and cook for 30 minutes or until the chicken is cooked through. Skim any scum and foam from the broth as the chicken cooks. Transfer the chicken to a bowl and discard the skin. Carefully pick the chicken from the bones and set aside. Discard the bones. Keep the broth on the stove over medium heat.

2. **Prepare the noodles:** Prepare the noodles according to package instructions in a large pot. Drain and rinse and set aside.

3. **Finish the broth:** Add the white and light green (not dark green) parts of the scallions to the broth. Next, add the cooked, shredded chicken, sliced squash, and the cabbage and turn the heat to medium. Cook until the squash is fork tender, about 10 minutes. Turn off the heat.

4. **To serve:** Divide the cooked noodles between bowls and ladle the broth on top. Arrange the chicken, squash, and cabbage on top of the noodles. Sprinkle each dish with sesame seeds and the dark green parts of the scallions. Add a drizzle of chili oil and sliced jalapeño, if desired. Enjoy!

Easy Cilantro-Lime Shrimp Salad

Time to Make: 30–40 minutes

Serves: 4

WHY THIS RECIPE WORKS

This easy cilantro-lime shrimp salad is bright, fresh, and spicy with just a hint of sweetness to offset the spices. It's a flavorful, low-carb dream dinner. The cilantro-lime dressing works well on both the shrimp and the salad, so you will use half the dressing on the shrimp as a marinade and half the dressing on top of the finished salad. If using a watermelon radish, peel it. If using red radishes, it is not necessary to peel them.

SUBSTITUTIONS

Shrimp: Extra-firm tofu, pressed and diced into cubes or boneless, skinless chicken breasts or thighs, cooking time will vary

EQUIPMENT & LEFTOVERS

You'll need: Food processor, zipper storage bag, large bowl, skillet

Leftovers: Do not dress any greens you do not intend to eat immediately. Store the tomato-cucumber salad and the shrimp separately in the fridge for up to 3 days and assemble the salads as desired!

INGREDIENTS

Cilantro-Lime Dressing:

¾ cup fresh cilantro

1–2 jalapeños, depending on heat preference, trimmed and chopped into thirds

4 cloves garlic, peeled

1 lime, juiced

½ cup extra-virgin olive oil

2 tablespoons honey, plus more to taste if desired

Salt and pepper to taste

Shrimp Salad:

1½ pounds large shrimp, peeled and deveined, tails left on or removed, depending on preference

3 Roma tomatoes, small-diced

½ cup fresh cilantro, finely chopped

1 jalapeño, trimmed and minced

1 English cucumber, small-diced

1 lime, juice

1 watermelon radish (or 5 red radishes), peeled and thinly sliced into half-moons

16 ounces baby greens

Salt and pepper to taste

1 teaspoon extra-virgin olive oil

1 tablespoon cooking oil

(Continued on next page)

METHOD

1. **Prepare cilantro-lime dressing:** In a food processor, combine all the ingredients for the cilantro-lime dressing and pulse until well-combined. If the dressing seems too thick, add a bit more oil or lime juice. Season with salt to taste. Set aside.

2. **Marinate the shrimp:** Transfer the shrimp to a bowl or zipper storage bag and pour in half the cilantro-lime dressing and toss to combine. Transfer to the refrigerator for 15 to 20 minutes.

3. **Prepare the tomato-cucumber salad:** In a bowl, combine the tomatoes, cilantro, minced jalapeño, diced cucumber, lime juice, and radish slices and toss to combine. Season with salt and pepper to taste.

4. **Dress the greens:** Transfer the greens to a large bowl and drizzle with extra-virgin olive oil. Add a sprinkle of salt and a touch of black pepper and use your hands to dress the greens with the oil. Divide the greens between plates and set aside.

5. **Cook the cilantro-lime shrimp:** Heat cooking oil in a large skillet over medium-high heat until very hot. Add shrimp in an even layer, cooking in batches if necessary, and pour 1 to 2 tablespoons of marinade from the bag over the shrimp. Discard any excess marinade from the bag. Cook for 1 to 2 minutes and then flip the shrimp and cook for 2 to 3 minutes more or until the shrimp are opaque and cooked through. Turn off the heat.

6. **To serve:** Pile the tomato-cucumber garnish on top of the salad greens and arrange the cooked shrimp on top. Drizzle with the remaining cilantro-lime dressing. Enjoy!

Spice-Rubbed Acorn Squash with Spicy Rice

Time to Make: 45 minutes

Serves: 4

WHY THIS RECIPE WORKS

Acorn squash is a great vessel for spices and seasonings. With its sweet, nutty, and mild flavor, it really lets the spices shine through in this recipe.

SUBSTITUTIONS

Acorn squash: Butternut squash, sweet potatoes, or boneless, skinless chicken breasts

EQUIPMENT & LEFTOVERS

You'll need: Saucepan with a lid, baking sheet, aluminum foil, wide sauté pan

Leftovers: Store leftovers in the fridge for up to 4 days

INGREDIENTS

1 cup uncooked brown, wild, or white rice (cook time may vary)

2 cups water

2 tablespoons plus 3 teaspoons cooking oil, divided

Salt to taste

2 tablespoons chili powder

1 tablespoon ground cumin

2 teaspoons ground black pepper

1 teaspoon onion powder

1 teaspoon dried oregano

1 teaspoon garlic powder

1 teaspoon paprika

1 acorn squash, halved lengthwise and seeds removed, each half thinly sliced

Pepper to taste

1 yellow onion, peeled and diced

1 red bell pepper, trimmed, deseeded, and diced

1 jalapeño, trimmed and diced

1 (14.5-ounce) can fire-roasted diced tomatoes

1 (15-ounce) can black beans, drained and rinsed

¼ cup fresh cilantro, roughly chopped

3 scallions, sliced

METHOD

1. **Prepare the rice:** Combine the rice with 2 cups water and 2 teaspoons cooking oil and a sprinkle of salt in a saucepan. Bring to a boil and then cover and reduce heat to very low. Simmer for 30 to 40 minutes or until the rice is tender. Turn off the heat and rest for 5 minutes before fluffing with a fork.

2. **Prepare the spice blend:** In a bowl, combine the chili powder, cumin, black pepper, onion powder, oregano, garlic powder, and paprika.

3. **Roast the squash:** Preheat oven to 400°F. Line a baking sheet with aluminum foil and arrange the squash in an even layer on the sheet. Drizzle 2 tablespoons of cooking oil, season with salt and pepper, and sprinkle half the spice blend over both sides of the acorn squash. Transfer squash to the oven and roast for 15 minutes. Flip and roast an additional 10 to 15 minutes or until tender. Set aside and keep warm.

4. **Prepare the spicy rice:** While the squash is roasting, heat the remaining 1 teaspoon cooking

(Continued on page 157)

oil in a wide sauté pan over medium-high heat. Add the diced onion, bell pepper, and jalapeño and cook for 5 to 6 minutes or until beginning to soften. Season with salt and pepper to taste. Add diced tomatoes, black beans, and the rest of the spice mixture. Pour in the cooked rice and toss to combine. Cover and cook for 10 minutes or until the vegetables are softened and the flavors have melded. Taste and season to your preferences.

5. **To serve:** Divide the rice between bowls and serve with sliced acorn squash on top. Garnish with the fresh cilantro and sliced scallions. Enjoy!

Pork Chops with Creamy Peas and Tomatoes

Time to Make: 30 minutes

Serves: 4

WHY THIS RECIPE WORKS

This recipe is so easy to prepare and is a perfect year-round recipe that can be adapted to each season. If fresh peas aren't available, use frozen peas or other in-season vegetables such as chopped asparagus, sugar snap peas, or even frozen edamame.

SUBSTITUTIONS

Pork chops: Thin chicken breasts

Green peas: Any seasonal green vegetable

EQUIPMENT & LEFTOVERS

You'll need: Oven-safe pan, meat thermometer

Leftovers: Store leftovers in the fridge for 3–4 days

INGREDIENTS

4 boneless pork chops, about 1½-inches thick

Salt and pepper to taste

1 tablespoon cooking oil

1 yellow onion, peeled and diced

4 cloves garlic, peeled and minced

2 tablespoons butter (optional)

1 pint cherry tomatoes, halved, or 1 (14.5-ounce) can diced tomatoes

2 cups low-sodium chicken stock

12 ounces fresh or frozen green peas

½ teaspoon crushed red pepper, optional

1 teaspoon dry thyme

½ cup heavy cream

1 lemon, juice

METHOD

1. **Prepare the pork chops:** Preheat oven to 400°F. Pat the pork chops dry and season all over with salt and pepper. In a wide oven-safe skillet or sauté pan, heat the cooking oil over medium-high heat. Once very hot, add the pork chops and cook for 3 minutes until very well-browned and crisping up around the edges. Flip and cook an additional 2 to 3 minutes. Transfer to the oven for 10 to 12 minutes or until the pork chops reach 140°F. Remove from the oven and cover loosely with foil to rest as you finish the rest of the recipe.

2. **Fry the aromatics:** Return the same pan to medium heat. Add the yellow onion and cook for 5 minutes. Next, add the garlic and cook for 45 seconds or until fragrant. Add the butter. Once the butter is melted and frothy, add the tomatoes and cook for 5 minutes. Season everything in the pan with salt and pepper.

3. **Cook the creamy peas and tomatoes:** Pour chicken stock into the pan and scrape up any browned bits stuck to the bottom of the pan. Add the peas and bring to a boil. Reduce heat and simmer for 5 minutes or until the peas are softened but still bright green. Return the heat to medium (a very low boil). Season to taste with salt and pepper and then add the crushed red pepper (if using) and thyme. Pour in the heavy cream and lemon juice. Cook for 5 additional minutes or until the sauce has thickened a bit. Turn off the heat.

4. **To serve:** Thinly slice the pork chops. Divide the creamy peas and tomatoes between bowls and arrange the sliced pork on top. Pour more of the cream sauce over the pork chops just before serving. Enjoy!

PLAN 3: WEEK 3

This seven-day recipe plan includes dinner recipes for five days, all of which serve four. To conquer the grocery store in one shopping trip, the next page outlines a detailed grocery list, with items separated by store department. You will also find storage, freezing, and thawing tips to help you plan your week. This plan's flavor profile is all about the combination of creamy, tangy, and herby. Crème fraîche adds subtle tang and richness to multiple recipes, while basil and parsley add herby brightness. Pay special attention to the key players (fresh basil, fresh parsley, and fresh cauliflower) throughout the week and be sure to buy the freshest and healthiest of those ingredients that you can find, because you will use them for multiple recipes. Store produce in a bag in the crisper to keep fresh.

THE MENU

MONDAY
Crispy-Skinned Trout with Sautéed
Leeks and Kale

TUESDAY
Roast Chicken with Cauliflower and
Caperberries

WEDNESDAY
Spinach Fettuccine with Basil Crème
Fraîche Sauce

THURSDAY
Chicken Meatballs with Orzo and
Vegetables

FRIDAY
Farmers' Market Salad with Roasted
Vegetables

FOOD SAFETY GUIDELINES

Buying groceries for the entire week can require some forethought, so be sure to refer to the FDA's storage and freezing guidelines for raw ingredients. All fish, chicken, and steak require twenty-four hours to thaw out in the fridge.

Raw fish, shellfish, chicken, and ground meats: Store in fridge for 1–2 days
Steak and pork (roasts and chops): Store in fridge for 3–5 days
Uncooked, unopened bacon: Store in fridge for 1–2 weeks

PROTEIN

- ☐ 1½ pound skin-on trout fillets
- ☐ 8 bone-in, skin-on chicken thighs
- ☐ 1 pound ground chicken
- ☐ 4 eggs

GRAIN

- ☐ 16 ounces fresh spinach fettuccine
- ☐ 1 cup dry whole-wheat orzo

OIL

- ☐ Cooking oil
- ☐ Extra-virgin olive oil

DAIRY

- ☐ 2 tablespoons butter
- ☐ 1 cup crème fraîche
- ☐ ¼ cup grated Parmesan cheese

STOCK

- ☐ 3 cups low-sodium vegetable stock
- ☐ 6 cups low-sodium chicken stock

FRUITS & VEGETABLES

- ☐ 2 leeks
- ☐ 1 bunch lacinato kale
- ☐ 1 red onion
- ☐ 1 yellow onion
- ☐ 2 heads cauliflower
- ☐ 4 cloves garlic
- ☐ 6 carrots
- ☐ 5 ounces baby spinach
- ☐ 1 cup basil leaves
- ☐ 1 cup parsley
- ☐ 12 ounces Brussels sprouts
- ☐ 5 red radishes
- ☐ 1 head romaine lettuce
- ☐ 1 lemon

(Continued on next page)

PANTRY & SPICES

- ☐ Panko
- ☐ Lemon pepper, optional
- ☐ Dry thyme
- ☐ Paprika
- ☐ Caperberries
- ☐ Dry parsley
- ☐ Crushed red pepper
- ☐ Garlic powder
- ☐ Onion powder
- ☐ Dry dill
- ☐ Capers
- ☐ Salt
- ☐ Pepper

TIP

To speed up the thawing process, place the frozen protein in a resealable storage bag and push out the air before sealing the bag. Place the bag in a bowl and run cold water over the bag. Fill the bowl with water and use a heavy jar (such as peanut butter) to keep the bag submerged below the water. Replace the water every ten minutes with more cold water. Alternatively, allow the water to run at a very slow rate. This will take anywhere from thirty minutes to an hour. Note: To keep bacteria from forming, the water must be at 40°F. If using standing water, do not allow the water to reach room temperature.

Crispy-Skinned Trout with Sautéed Leeks and Kale

Time to Make: 30–35 minutes

Serves: 4

WHY THIS RECIPE WORKS

Crispy trout works well with buttery leeks and kale in this simple low-carb dinner recipe. This recipe is versatile and easy to swap ingredients depending on what you have on hand or what's available at your grocery store.

SUBSTITUTIONS

Trout: Skin-on salmon

Leeks: Vidalia onions

Lacinato kale: Baby spinach, arugula, swiss chard, or cabbage

EQUIPMENT & LEFTOVERS

You'll need: 2 skillets, paper towel, aluminum foil

Leftovers: Store leftovers in the fridge for up to 3 days

INGREDIENTS

2 tablespoons butter

2 leeks, trimmed and tough outer leaves removed, thoroughly washed and thinly sliced

1½ pound skin-on trout fillets, cut into 4 equal portions

Salt and pepper to taste

Lemon pepper, optional

2 tablespoons cooking oil

2 cups low-sodium vegetable stock

1 bunch lacinato kale, thick center rib removed and leaves torn into bite-size pieces

Extra-virgin olive oil, optional, for serving

(Continued on page 165)

METHOD

1. **Sauté leeks:** In a skillet, heat butter over medium-high until melted and frothy. Add the leeks and cook, stirring regularly, until very soft, about 10 to 12 minutes.

2. **Prepare the fish:** While the leeks are cooking, pat the trout fillets dry and season all over with salt, pepper, and lemon pepper (if using). In a skillet, heat 2 tablespoons cooking oil until very hot. Add 2 trout fillets, skin-side down, and cook for 2 to 3 minutes or until the skin is very crispy and releases from the pan easily. Flip and cook an additional 2 to 3 minutes or until the fish is cooked through. Cooking time will depend on the thickness of the fillets. Remove the fish and place on a serving plate, skin-side up, and cover with aluminum foil. Prepare the remaining 2 trout portions and transfer to the serving plate and keep warm.

3. **Finish cooking leeks:** Pour the vegetable stock into the skillet with the leeks and scrape up anything stuck to the bottom. Add the kale leaves and stir to incorporate. Once the kale leaves have wilted, season with salt and pepper and turn off the heat.

4. **To serve:** Spoon leeks and kale into shallow bowls and serve with a trout fillet on top. Drizzle with a touch of extra-virgin olive oil, if desired. Enjoy!

Roast Chicken with Cauliflower and Caperberries

Time to Make: 55 minutes

Serves: 4

WHY THIS RECIPE WORKS

This roast chicken is an exciting take on a simple chicken dinner. Because caperberries are little flavor bombs, they add a bit of complexity with their briny saltiness to this otherwise very simple dish.

SUBSTITUTIONS

Chicken: Bone-in pork chops or boneless chicken breasts, cooking time will vary

Cauliflower: Peeled, diced potatoes

Caperberries: 2 tablespoons drained, rinsed capers

EQUIPMENT & LEFTOVERS

You'll need: Wide sauté pan or braising pot, meat thermometer

Leftovers: Store leftovers in the fridge for 3–4 days

INGREDIENTS

8 bone-in, skin-on chicken thighs

Salt and pepper to taste

1 tablespoon cooking oil

1 red onion, peeled and sliced into thin wedges

1 head of cauliflower, trimmed and cut into florets

1 teaspoon dry thyme

1 teaspoon paprika

Crushed red pepper to taste

¼ cup caperberries, drained and rinsed

1 tablespoon dry parsley, plus more for garnish

METHOD

1. **Preheat oven to 425°F.**

2. **Prepare the chicken:** Pat the chicken dry and season all over with salt and pepper. In a wide sauté pan or braising pot, heat the oil over medium-high. Add the chicken, skin-side down, and cook for 5 to 7 minutes without moving or until the skin is golden brown and very crispy. Flip and cook 1 to 2 minutes. Transfer to a plate. Note: Do not overcrowd the pan; cook the chicken in batches if needed.

3. **Sauté the vegetables:** Drain off all but 1 tablespoon of fat from the pan and return the heat to medium-high. Add the onion and cook for 2 to 3 minutes or until it begins to soften. Add the cauliflower and toss with the onion. Season the cauliflower and onion with salt, pepper, thyme, paprika, and crushed red pepper. Cook for 5 more minutes or until the cauliflower begins to soften just a bit.

4. **Roast the chicken with cauliflower:** Nestle the chicken into the cauliflower (or transfer all vegetables to a roasting sheet and place the chicken on top). Transfer to the oven for 30 minutes or until the cauliflower is cooked through and beginning to char and the chicken reaches 165°F on an instant-read meat thermometer. Transfer the pan back to the stovetop. Return pan to medium heat and add the caperberries and dry parsley. Cook for 1 to 2 minutes. (If using a sheet pan, simply toss the caperberries and dry parsley with the cauliflower and return to the oven for 2 to 3 minutes.)

5. **To serve:** Divide the cauliflower and caperberries between plates and place a chicken thigh on top. Garnish with a pinch of dry parsley, if desired. Enjoy!

Spinach Fettuccine with Basil Crème Fraîche Sauce

Time to Make: 25 minutes

Serves: 4

WHY THIS RECIPE WORKS

This spinach fettuccine is tossed in an herby, fresh sauce that has just the right amount of tang from crème fraîche.

SUBSTITUTIONS

Spinach fettuccine: Whole-wheat or spinach pasta of your choice

Crème fraîche: Sour cream or Greek yogurt

EQUIPMENT & LEFTOVERS

You'll need: Large pot, wide skillet

Leftovers: Store leftovers in the fridge for 3–4 days

INGREDIENTS

16 ounces fresh spinach fettuccine

1 teaspoon cooking oil

4 cloves garlic, peeled and minced

½ teaspoon crushed red pepper

1 cup low-sodium vegetable stock

½ cup crème fraîche

½ cup fresh basil leaves, torn

Pepper to taste

METHOD

1. **Prepare the fettuccine:** Bring a large pot of salted water to a boil. Cook the fettuccine according to package instructions and reserve ½ cup cooking water.

2. **Prepare the sauce:** In a wide skillet, heat 1 teaspoon oil over medium heat until hot. Add garlic and crushed red pepper and cook until fragrant, about 30 seconds, being careful not to burn the garlic. Add vegetable stock and bring to a boil.

3. **Prepare the crème fraîche sauce:** Add the crème fraîche to the reserved warm pasta cooking water and whisk until smooth. Add this mixture to the skillet and stir to combine. Cook for 5 to 10 minutes or until the sauce is reduced slightly and thickened.

4. **Finish the pasta:** Add the torn basil leaves to the sauce and cook for 1 minute or until just wilted. Toss the cooked fettuccine with the sauce for about 1 to 2 minutes. After 1 to 2 minutes, the pasta should be glossy and well-coated with the sauce. Turn off the heat.

5. **To serve:** Divide the fettuccine between bowls and sprinkle with black pepper if desired. Enjoy!

Chicken Meatballs with Orzo and Vegetables

Time to Make: 45 minutes

Serves: 4

WHY THIS RECIPE WORKS

Use up the last of the crème fraîche with this recipe for juicy chicken meatballs and an aromatic broth with orzo.

SUBSTITUTIONS

Ground: Ground turkey or ground pork

Orzo: Any small pasta, such as ditalini or acini de pepe

Crème fraîche: Sour cream or Greek yogurt

EQUIPMENT & LEFTOVERS

You'll need: Wide pot

Leftovers: Store leftovers in the fridge for 3–4 days

INGREDIENTS

1 pound ground chicken

½ cup crème fraîche

½ cup panko, more if needed

1 teaspoon garlic powder

½ teaspoon onion powder

½ teaspoon dry dill

Salt and pepper to taste

1 tablespoon cooking oil, plus more if necessary

1 yellow onion, peeled and diced

4 carrots, peeled and sliced into rounds

6 cups low-sodium chicken stock

1 teaspoon dry thyme

Crushed red pepper to taste

1 cup dry whole-wheat orzo

5 ounces baby spinach

½ cup basil leaves, roughly chopped

½ cup parsley, roughly chopped, with a pinch reserved for garnish

METHOD

1. **Prepare the chicken meatballs:** In a bowl, combine the ground chicken, crème fraîche, panko, garlic powder, onion powder, dry dill, salt, and pepper. Using your hands, gently mix until just combined. Form into tablespoon-sized meatballs and transfer to a plate. Refrigerate until ready to cook.

2. **Cook meatballs:** In a wide pot, heat 1 tablespoon oil over medium-high until hot. Add the meatballs in an even layer and cook until well-browned all over, about 6 to 8 minutes. The meatballs do not need to be fully cooked through. Transfer to a plate.

3. **Prepare the broth:** If the skillet seems dry, add a touch more cooking oil. Add diced onion and sliced carrots and cook until softened and brown, about 5 minutes. Pour in the chicken stock and bring to a boil. Add meatballs and cook for 12 to 15 minutes or until the meatballs are fully cooked through and the carrots are tender. Season with thyme, salt, pepper, and crushed red pepper to taste. Bring the broth back to a boil and pour in the orzo, stirring the broth frequently to keep the orzo from sticking. Cook, stirring often, for 7 minutes or until just under al dente. Right before the orzo has finished cooking, stir in the spinach, basil, and all but the reserved fresh parsley. Cook for 2 to 3 more minutes or until the spinach is wilted and orzo is tender. Turn off the heat.

4. **To serve:** Ladle the orzo and broth into shallow bowls and serve with the chicken meatballs. Sprinkle the reserved parsley on top. Enjoy!

Farmers' Market Salad with Roasted Vegetables

Time to Make: 35 minutes

Serves: 4

WHY THIS RECIPE WORKS

Because this salad is the ideal vessel for leftover herbs and root vegetables, it's the perfect recipe to round out the week.

SUBSTITUTIONS

Brussels sprouts: Asparagus or sugar snap peas

Radishes: Turnip or rutabaga

Carrots: Sweet potatoes or butternut squash

Romaine lettuce: Any leafy green

EQUIPMENT & LEFTOVERS

You'll need: Baking sheet, saucepan, whisk, zester

Leftovers: Store leftovers in the fridge for 3–4 days

INGREDIENTS

12 ounces Brussels sprouts, trimmed and halved

5 red radishes, trimmed and quartered

2 carrots, peeled and sliced into rounds

1 small head cauliflower, trimmed, cored, and cut into florets

¼ cup plus 2 tablespoons extra-virgin olive oil, divided

Salt and pepper to taste

1 lemon, juice and zest

1 tablespoon capers, drained

¼ cup grated Parmesan cheese, plus more for serving

Crushed red pepper to taste

4 eggs

1 head romaine lettuce, roughly chopped

½ cup fresh parsley, roughly chopped

METHOD

1. **Roast the vegetables:** Preheat oven to 425°F. Toss the Brussels sprouts, radishes, carrots, and cauliflower with 2 tablespoons extra-virgin olive oil on a baking sheet and arrange the vegetables in an even layer. Season with salt and pepper. Transfer to the oven and roast for 25 minutes or until well-browned and tender, flipping once halfway through cooking.

2. **Prepare the dressing:** While the vegetables are roasting, combine the lemon juice and zest and capers in a bowl. Add the Parmesan cheese. Slowly add the remaining ¼ cup extra-virgin olive oil, whisking to incorporate until smooth. Taste and season with salt, pepper, and crushed red pepper to taste.

3. **Prepare the jammy eggs:** Bring a saucepan of water to a boil. Add the eggs and cover. Cook for 6 minutes. Run the eggs under cold water and crack the shells gently all over with the side of a spoon. Peel and set aside.

4. **Dress the greens:** Toss chopped romaine lettuce with chopped parsley and half the dressing.

5. **To serve:** Divide the dressed greens between salad bowls and pile the warm, roasted vegetables on top. Nestle the soft-boiled eggs into the salad and sprinkle a bit of parmesan cheese on top, if desired. Serve with the remaining dressing and enjoy!

PLAN 3: WEEK 4

This seven-day recipe plan includes dinner recipes for five days, all of which serve four. To conquer the grocery store in one shopping trip, the next page outlines a detailed grocery list, with items separated by store department. You will also find storage, freezing, and thawing tips to help you plan your week. This plan is sweet and bright, utilizing the balance of sugar and citrus or acidity in multiple recipes for balanced meals that won't teeter too far in either direction. Pay special attention to the key players (fresh parsley and citrus fruit) throughout the week and be sure to buy the freshest and healthiest of those ingredients that you can find, because you will use them for multiple recipes. Store produce in the crisper to keep it fresh.

THE MENU

MONDAY
Gnocchi with Parsley-Pepita Pesto

TUESDAY
Maple-Sage Japanese Sweet Potatoes and Pork

WEDNESDAY
Seared Endive Salad with Caramelized Onions

THURSDAY
Spicy Shiitake Mushroom and Soft Tofu Soup

FRIDAY
Lemon-Roasted Chicken with Chickpeas and Brown Rice

PLAN 3: WEEK 4
CONQUERING THE GROCERY STORE

FOOD SAFETY GUIDELINES

Buying groceries for the entire week can require some forethought, so be sure to refer to the FDA's storage and freezing guidelines for raw ingredients. All fish, chicken, and steak require twenty-four hours to thaw out in the fridge.

Raw fish, shellfish, chicken, and ground meats: Store in fridge for 1–2 days
Steak and pork (roasts and chops): Store in fridge for 3–5 days
Uncooked, unopened bacon: Store in fridge for 1–2 weeks

PROTEIN

- ☐ 1 pound pork tenderloin
- ☐ 16 ounces soft tofu
- ☐ 4 boneless, skinless chicken breasts

GRAIN

- ☐ 16 ounces fresh or frozen gnocchi
- ☐ 1 cup uncooked white rice
- ☐ 2 cups uncooked brown or wild rice

OIL

- ☐ Cooking oil
- ☐ Extra-virgin olive oil

DAIRY

- ☐ ⅔ cup grated parmesan cheese
- ☐ 2 tablespoons butter

STOCK

- ☐ 5 cups low-sodium vegetable stock
- ☐ 1 cup low-sodium chicken stock

FRUITS & VEGETABLES

- ☐ 5 scallions
- ☐ 2½ cups fresh parsley
- ☐ 2 yellow onions
- ☐ 2 Vidalia onions
- ☐ 11 cloves garlic
- ☐ 10 ounces fresh or frozen peas
- ☐ ½ ounce fresh sage leaves
- ☐ 1 orange
- ☐ 4 small Japanese sweet potatoes
- ☐ 10 ounces baby greens
- ☐ 16 ounces baby spinach
- ☐ 1 pint cherry tomatoes
- ☐ 4 Belgian endives
- ☐ 1 lemon
- ☐ 8 ounces shiitake mushrooms
- ☐ 1 serrano pepper, optional
- ☐ Fresh cilantro leaves, optional

(Continued on next page)

PANTRY & SPICES

- ☐ 2 (15-ounce) cans chickpeas
- ☐ 1 cup pumpkin seeds
- ☐ ¼ cup maple syrup
- ☐ Sugar
- ☐ Sesame oil
- ☐ Gochugaru
- ☐ Gochujang
- ☐ Soy sauce
- ☐ Sesame seeds
- ☐ Cumin
- ☐ Paprika
- ☐ Garlic powder
- ☐ Cayenne powder
- ☐ Salt
- ☐ Pepper
- ☐ Crushed red pepper

TIP

To speed up the thawing process, place the frozen protein in a resealable storage bag and push out the air before sealing the bag. Place the bag in a bowl and run cold water over the bag. Fill the bowl with water and use a heavy jar (such as peanut butter) to keep the bag submerged below the water. Replace the water every ten minutes with more cold water. Alternatively, allow the water to run at a very slow rate. This will take anywhere from thirty minutes to an hour. Note: To keep bacteria from forming, the water must be at 40°F. If using standing water, do not allow the water to reach room temperature.

Gnocchi with Parsley-Pepita Pesto

Time to Make: 30 minutes

Serves: 4

WHY THIS RECIPE WORKS

Preparing homemade gnocchi isn't super challenging, but when it's Monday night, the last thing you want to be doing is flouring surfaces in your kitchen. Using store-bought gnocchi will still land you on a delicious dinner that's quick and easy to prepare. The parsley-pepita pesto is an exciting take on traditional basil pesto. Pepitas (pumpkin seeds) are an extremely affordable option to pine nuts and still add a nice nuttiness to the pesto.

SUBSTITUTIONS

Gnocchi: Pearled couscous (cook time may vary)

Frozen peas: Fresh or frozen broccoli, fresh asparagus, or sugar snap peas

Pepitas: Sunflower seeds, squash seeds, or walnuts

EQUIPMENT & LEFTOVERS

You'll need: Large pot, wide skillet, food processor

Leftovers: Store leftovers in the fridge for 3–4 days

INGREDIENTS

Gnocchi:

16 ounces fresh or frozen gnocchi

2 tablespoons butter

1 tablespoon extra-virgin olive oil

1 yellow onion, peeled and diced

3 cloves garlic, peeled and minced

1 cup vegetable stock

Salt, pepper, and crushed red pepper to taste

8 ounces fresh or frozen peas, thawed

Fresh parsley leaves, for garnish

Parmesan cheese, grated, for garnish

Parsley-Pepita Pesto:

2 cups fresh parsley, trimmed, a few leaves reserved for garnish

4 cloves garlic, peeled

1 cup pumpkin seeds

⅓ cup grated parmesan cheese, plus more for garnish

Salt, pepper, and crushed red pepper to taste

⅓ cup extra-virgin olive oil

METHOD

1. **Cook the gnocchi:** Bring a large pot of water to a boil. Add the gnocchi and boil for 2 to 3 minutes until slightly under al dente. Drain and rinse and set aside.

2. **Prepare the pesto:** Combine all the ingredients for the pesto in a food processor except the extra-virgin olive oil and pulse until finely grated. Add the oil and continue pulsing until well-combined. Taste and season to your preferences. Set aside.

3. **Fry the gnocchi:** Add the butter to a wide skillet and turn the heat to medium-high. Once the butter is melted and frothy, add the gnocchi and cook, stirring occasionally, for 5 minutes until golden brown all over. Transfer the cooked gnocchi to a bowl.

(Continued on page 179)

4. **Cook the aromatics:** Add 1 tablespoon extra-virgin olive oil to the hot skillet. Once shimmering, add diced onion and cook, stirring regularly, for 6 minutes or until softened and golden brown. Add garlic and cook until fragrant, about 45 seconds. Pour in the vegetable stock and scrape up any food stuck to the bottom. Bring to a boil and season with salt, pepper, and crushed red pepper. Boil for 5 minutes until reduced by half. Add the pesto and the peas to the skillet and cook for 3–4 minutes, stirring continuously to incorporate the pesto into the sauce.

5. **Finish the gnocchi:** Add the gnocchi and toss to combine. Cook for 2 minutes to allow the gnocchi to absorb the pesto sauce. Taste and season to your preferences.

6. **To serve:** Spoon the gnocchi into shallow bowls and garnish with a few parsley leaves and grated parmesan, if desired. Enjoy!

Maple-Sage Japanese Sweet Potatoes and Pork

Time to Make: 30 minutes

Serves: 4

WHY THIS RECIPE WORKS

In this sweet and citrusy salad recipe, pork tenderloin and Japanese sweet potatoes are roasted in an orange and maple-sage sauce and placed atop tender greens for a salad that is equal parts light and refreshing yet warm and comforting.

SUBSTITUTIONS

Pork tenderloin: Boneless skinless chicken breasts or pork chops (cook time may vary) or omit for a vegan option

Japanese sweet potatoes: Baby sweet potatoes, diced butternut squash, or sliced acorn squash

Fresh sage: Fresh tarragon, or omit

EQUIPMENT & LEFTOVERS

You'll need: Wide oven-safe skillet, meat thermometer, zester

Leftovers: Pork and sweet potatoes can be stored in the fridge for 3–4 days. Dressed greens should be enjoyed immediately.

INGREDIENTS

¼ cup maple syrup

½ ounce fresh sage leaves

1 orange, juice and zest (zest reserved for garnish)

1 tablespoon cooking oil, plus more if necessary

4 small Japanese sweet potatoes, halved

1 pound pork tenderloin

Salt and pepper to taste

10 ounces baby greens

2 teaspoons extra-virgin olive oil

METHOD

1. **Prepare the sauce:** In a bowl, combine the maple syrup, sage leaves, and orange juice and stir to combine.

2. **Sear the sweet potatoes:** Preheat oven to 400°F. Heat 1 tablespoon cooking oil in a wide oven-safe skillet over medium-high heat. Add sweet potatoes, cut-side down, and cook without moving for 3 to 4 minutes or until browned all over. Flip and cook an additional 1 to 2 minutes. Using tongs, transfer the potatoes to a plate.

3. **Prepare the pork:** If the skillet seems dry, add an additional teaspoon of oil over medium-high heat. Pat the pork dry and season all over with salt and pepper. Once hot, add the pork tenderloin and cook for 3–4 minutes per side until well-browned all over. Pour the sauce into the skillet and spoon it all over the pork. Turn off the heat. Arrange the sweet potatoes around the pork and spoon the sauce over the sweet potatoes. Transfer to the oven for 12 to 15 minutes or until an instant-read thermometer reaches 140–145°F for medium rare. Remove the skillet from the oven. Transfer the cooked pork to a cutting board and rest for 5 minutes before slicing.

4. **Prepare the greens:** While the pork is roasting, toss the greens with 2 teaspoons extra-virgin olive oil and a sprinkle of salt and pepper.

5. **To serve:** Divide the greens between plates and serve with sweet potatoes and sliced pork. Spoon any extra sauce from the pan over the dish and garnish with the reserved orange zest. Enjoy!

Seared Endive Salad with Caramelized Onions

Time to Make: 40

Serves: 4

WHY THIS RECIPE WORKS

Endives are mellow and sweet when cooked, which make them a perfect match for slightly acidic cherry tomatoes.

SUBSTITUTIONS

Endives: Radicchio or escarole

Cherry tomatoes: Any fresh tomato variety

Baby spinach: Any leafy salad green

Parmesan cheese: Crumbled goat cheese or feta cheese

EQUIPMENT & LEFTOVERS

You'll Need: Skillet

Leftovers: This salad should be enjoyed immediately

INGREDIENTS

3 tablespoons cooking oil, divided

2 Vidalia onions, peeled and thinly sliced

Salt to taste

1 teaspoon sugar, optional

16 ounces baby spinach

1 pint cherry tomatoes, halved

⅓ cup grated parmesan cheese, optional

2 teaspoons extra-virgin olive oil

Pepper to taste

4 Belgian endives, halved

METHOD

1. **Caramelize the onions:** In a skillet, heat 2 tablespoons cooking oil over medium-high heat until very hot. Add the onions and sprinkle with salt and 1 teaspoon sugar, if desired. Cook, stirring often until the liquid has evaporated and the onions have begun to turn golden brown, about 15 minutes. Cook an additional 15 minutes or until the onions turn a deep golden brown. Adjust the heat as necessary to keep the onions from burning and stir them often. Transfer the onions to a serving platter and keep warm.

2. **Prepare the salad:** Five minutes before the onions have finished caramelizing, toss spinach with cherry tomatoes, parmesan cheese, extra-virgin olive oil, and a sprinkle of salt and pepper. Divide between 4 plates. Heat the remaining 1 tablespoon oil in the skillet over medium-high heat. Add the endives, cut-side down, and cook without moving for 2 to 3 minutes or until well-browned. Flip and cook an additional 1 to 2 minutes or until they've begun to soften slightly. Note: Do not overcrowd the skillet; cook in batches if necessary. Transfer to a plate and sprinkle salt over the endives.

3. **To serve:** Pile the caramelized onions on top of each salad and serve with the seared endives on top. Enjoy!

Spicy Shiitake Mushroom and Soft Tofu Soup

Time to Make: 35–40 minutes

Serves: 4

WHY THIS RECIPE WORKS

Soft tofu soup is a spicy, warming, yet surprisingly rich Korean soup. This tofu soup is loaded with shiitake mushrooms and plenty of gochujang. Reduce the gochujang and gochugaru if you want to control the heat. If you cannot find gochujang or gochugaru at your grocery store, you can omit and add heat with sriracha to the stock. It won't be exactly like soft tofu soup, but it will still taste delicious!

SUBSTITUTIONS

Shiitake mushrooms: Any mushroom variety will work

EQUIPMENT & LEFTOVERS

You'll Need: Soup pot, saucepan with a lid

Leftovers: Store leftovers in the fridge for 3–4 days

INGREDIENTS

1 tablespoon sesame oil

1 yellow onion, peeled and diced

4 garlic cloves, peeled and minced

2 teaspoons gochugaru

⅓ cup gochujang

2 tablespoons soy sauce

4 cups low-sodium vegetable stock

8 ounces shiitake mushrooms, caps sliced and stems discarded

1 cup uncooked white rice

2 cups water

1 teaspoon sesame seeds

16 ounces soft tofu

Fresh cilantro leaves, optional, for serving

1 serrano pepper, thinly sliced, optional, for serving

METHOD

1. **Prepare the soup base:** Heat 1 tablespoon sesame oil over medium-high heat in a soup pot. Add diced onion and cook, stirring often, for 3 to 4 minutes until the onion begins to soften. Add garlic and cook until fragrant. Add the gochugaru to the pot and cook for 1 to 2 minutes or until it is fragrant and begins to deepen in color. Add the gochujang to the pot along with the soy sauce and vegetable stock. Add the mushrooms. Bring to a boil and cook for 15 to 20 minutes or until the mushrooms are soft. Taste and season to your preferences.

2. **Prepare the rice:** As the soup is cooking, combine 1 cup rice with 2 cups of water and a sprinkle of salt in a saucepan. Bring to a boil and then cover and reduce heat to very low. Cook for 15 minutes before turning off the heat. Rest for 5 minutes. Fluff the rice and sprinkle with 1 teaspoon sesame seeds.

3. **Finish the soup:** Break the tofu into big pieces and add them to the soup, stirring to just incorporate into the broth. Cook for 3 minutes more.

4. **To serve:** Ladle the soup into bowls and garnish with fresh cilantro leaves and sliced serrano pepper, if using. Serve with white rice on the side. Enjoy!

Lemon-Roasted Chicken with Chickpeas and Brown Rice

Time to Make: 40 minutes

Serves: 4

WHY THIS RECIPE WORKS

Fresh herbs along with lemon juice and zest create bright, flavorful chickpeas, and a quick roast with the chicken ensures that you don't lose the zip from the lemon and herbs.

SUBSTITUTIONS

Chicken breasts: Cod, boneless pork chops, tempeh, or sweet potato rounds (cook times may vary)

Chickpeas: Cannellini beans or navy beans

EQUIPMENT & LEFTOVERS

You'll need: Small pot with lid, large bowl, paper towels, oven-safe skillet, zester, meat thermometer

Leftovers: Store in the fridge for up to 3 days

INGREDIENTS

2 cups uncooked brown or wild rice

3⅓ cups water

2 (15-ounce) cans chickpeas, drained and rinsed

1 lemon, juice and zest

½ cup fresh parsley, minced, a pinch reserved for garnish

5 scallions, trimmed and minced, a pinch reserved for garnish

2 teaspoons cumin, divided

2 teaspoons paprika, divided

1 teaspoon garlic powder, divided

Cayenne powder to taste

Salt and pepper to taste

4 boneless, skinless chicken breasts

1 tablespoon cooking oil

1 cup low-sodium chicken stock

Extra-virgin olive oil, optional, for serving

(Continued on next page)

METHOD

1. **Prepare rice:** Combine the rice with 3⅓ cups water and a teaspoon of salt. Bring to a boil and then stir once. Reduce heat to low, cover, and simmer for 30 minutes. Turn off the heat and allow to rest, covered, for 5 minutes before fluffing with a fork. Note: Cooking instructions may vary depending on rice variety.

2. **Prepare the chickpeas:** Transfer chickpeas to a large bowl with the lemon juice and zest, parsley, and scallions. Season with 1 teaspoon cumin, 1 teaspoon paprika, ½ teaspoon garlic powder, and a few dashes of cayenne powder. Season with salt and pepper to taste and toss to coat.

3. **Prepare the chicken:** Pat the chicken dry and transfer to a bowl. Season all over with salt and pepper. Add the remaining 1 teaspoon cumin, 1 teaspoon paprika, ½ teaspoon garlic powder, and a few dashes of cayenne powder. Toss to evenly coat.

4. **Sauté the chicken:** Heat 1 tablespoon oil in an oven-safe skillet. Add the chicken breasts and cook for 5 minutes per side until well-browned. Transfer the chicken to a plate.

5. **Finish the dish:** Pour in the chicken stock and scrape up any browned bits stuck to the bottom of the skillet. Add the chickpeas and chicken breasts and transfer to the oven for 10 to 12 minutes or until the chicken reaches 165°F.

6. **To serve:** Divide the cooked rice between plates and spoon the chickpeas on top. Serve with a chicken breast on each dish. Sprinkle with reserved parsley and scallions. Drizzle with a touch of extra-virgin olive oil, if desired. Enjoy!

About the Author

Kylie Perrotti is a Baltimore-based, self-taught home cooking enthusiast and art director. She found her passion for cooking as a kid in the kitchen with her parents, and she found her love of food photography when she began photographing for magazines while living in New York City. She started her website triedandtruerecipe.com because she wanted a no-frills, no-nonsense approach to finding easy, elegant, delicious meals to make at home.

After moving back to Baltimore, she expanded her passion for cooking to building community and started the Baltimore Supper Club, a communal and inclusive cooking and food education club in the Baltimore Metro Area whose mission is to connect Baltimore residents over a unified love of cooking. The club is for cooks of all levels who want to enhance their palate and cooking skills through an active and supportive online community, themed dinner parties, and food education events in Baltimore.

Conversion Charts

Metric and Imperial Conversions

(These conversions are rounded for convenience)

Ingredient	Cups/Tablespoons/ Teaspoons	Ounces	Grams/Milliliters
Butter	1 cup/ 16 tablespoons/ 2 sticks	8 ounces	230 grams
Cheese, shredded	1 cup	4 ounces	110 grams
Cream cheese	1 tablespoon	0.5 ounce	14.5 grams
Cornstarch	1 tablespoon	0.3 ounce	8 grams
Flour, all-purpose	1 cup/1 tablespoon	4.5 ounces/0.3 ounce	125 grams/8 grams
Flour, whole wheat	1 cup	4 ounces	120 grams
Fruit, dried	1 cup	4 ounces	120 grams
Fruits or veggies, chopped	1 cup	5 to 7 ounces	145 to 200 grams
Fruits or veggies, pureed	1 cup	8.5 ounces	245 grams
Honey, maple syrup, or corn syrup	1 tablespoon	0.75 ounce	20 grams
Liquids: cream, milk, water, or juice	1 cup	8 fluid ounces	240 milliliters
Oats	1 cup	5.5 ounces	150 grams
Salt	1 teaspoon	0.2 ounce	6 grams
Spices: cinnamon, cloves, ginger, or nutmeg (ground)	1 teaspoon	0.2 ounce	5 milliliters
Sugar, brown, firmly packed	1 cup	7 ounces	200 grams
Sugar, white	1 cup/1 tablespoon	7 ounces/0.5 ounce	200 grams/12.5 grams
Vanilla extract	1 teaspoon	0.2 ounce	4 grams

Oven Temperatures

Fahrenheit	Celsius	Gas Mark
225°	110°	¼
250°	120°	½
275°	140°	1
300°	150°	2
325°	160°	3
350°	180°	4
375°	190°	5
400°	200°	6
425°	220°	7
450°	230°	8

Index